TREASURING GOD *in Our* TRADITIONS

TREASURING
GOD *in Our*
TRADITIONS

NOËL PIPER

FOREWORD AND POETRY BY
JOHN PIPER

CROSSWAY BOOKS
WHEATON, ILLINOIS

Treasuring God in Our Traditions
Copyright © 2003 by Noël Piper
Published by Crossway Books
        a publishing ministry of Good News Publishers
        1300 Crescent Street
        Wheaton, Illinois 60187

Cover design: Christopher Gilbert / The DesignWorks Group, www.thedesignworksgroup.com
Cover illustration: Nicholas Wilton
Interior photos: SuperStock, Inc.
First printing 2003
Printed in the United States of America

First trade paper edition, 2007

Scripture verses are taken from *The Holy Bible: English Standard Version*® unless otherwise identified. Copyright © 2001 by Good News Publishers. Used by permission. All rights reserved.

Scripture quotations marked NASB are taken from the *New American Standard Bible*®. Copyright © The Lockman Foundation 1960, 1962, 1963, 1968, 1971, 1972, 1973, 1975, 1977. Used by permission. (www.Lockman.org)

Scripture quotations taken from the *Revised Standard Version* are identified RSV. Copyright © 1946, 1953 1971, 1973 by the Division of Christian Education of the National Council of the Churches of Christ in the U.S.A.

Scripture references marked KJV are taken from the King James Version.

ISBN 978-1-58134-833-0

Library of Congress Cataloging-in-Publication Data

Piper, Noël, 1947–
    Treasuring God in our traditions / Noël Piper; foreword and poems by John Piper.
        p.   cm.
    Includes bibliographical references.
        ISBN 1-58134-508-9 (alk. paper)
    1. Family—Religious aspects—Christianity. 2. Tradition (Theology) I. Piper, John, 1946– II. Title.
    BT707.7.P57 2003
    249—dc21

                                          2003007393

L B   16 15 14 13 12 11
15 14 13 12 11 10 9 8 7 6 5 4 3

Dedication

The bark deep-creased with age; the limbs
Were laden down with love, and hymns
Were heard beneath when wind bestirred
The bowing branches with the Word
Of heaven. O there were years of shade!

John Piper

With gratitude for my beloved "bowing branches":
Uncle Homer and Aunt Edna
Uncle James and Aunt Mary
Uncle Sam and Aunt Alice
Uncle Buddy and Aunt Lou Ellen
Uncle Hollis and Aunt Rachel
Uncle Zach and Aunt Norma
Uncle Hal and Aunt Ada Sue
Uncle Roy and Aunt Lou

And especially for
Daddy and Mother,
George and Pamela Henry

CONTENTS

FOREWORD

I love to read my wife's writing. It's just like her: velvet steel. Yes, there's a woman's touch. She is one. But there's also an edge because she believes in solid Truth.

Long ago we settled it: Manhood and womanhood are different—deeply, maddeningly, and blissfully different. That's not surprising. But we also agreed on something unexpected. What makes the most admirable women admirable, and the most noble men noble, is the touch that each has of the other's peculiarity. A rugged man with no "female" tenderness is less a man, and a nurturing woman with no "male" ruggedness is less a woman. So it stopped bothering us that I am the emotional, poetic, expressive one in this marriage, and she is the no-nonsense, suck-it-up, thick-skinned doer.

You will hear that, and, I predict, you will like it.

I have called our marriage and our home a matrix of Christian hedonism. Yes, four sons were conceived here and one daughter adopted. But our marriage has also been the birthplace of ideas. Or better: the birthplace of vision—seeing God as all-sovereign and all-satisfying. Woven into our family life is the conviction that God is most glorified in us when we are most satisfied in him. His glory and our joy are not at odds. In this matrix the vision matured; then it shaped everything.

Treasuring God in Our Traditions is exactly the right title for this book. God is the treasure of our lives. We see him in everything. We believe with all our hearts that "from him and through him and to him are all things." He gets the glory, we get the joy. My job has been to articulate the vision in writing. Noël has shaped a family around it. Now she turns that work into words.

I pray that this glimpse into our lengthening marriage (we were married in 1968) and into our family history—struggles and all—will clarify for you the biblical vision of the God that we love. Long ago we agreed that our family exists to spread a passion for God's supremacy in all things for the joy of all peoples through Jesus Christ. Now, if you wish, you may see a few more of the "all things" where we long to make God supreme. We have not "arrived." The banner over our lives is "Desiring God and Longing to Love," not "Always Full of Joy in God and Living Radically as a Result."

In this story, as with all stories, test all things and hold fast to what is good. Learn from our mistakes. Adapt some of our imperfect successes. Mainly, look for the Treasure. His grace is everywhere. We could not have made it this far without him. He will not be hard to find. And when you find him, give thanks that he found you first.

FOREWORD

heir·loom
Pronunciation: 'ar-lüm, 'er-lüm
Something of special value handed on
from one generation to another.

ONE

HEIRLOOMS

Dear Mother,

What kind of fur is the coat you got when you lived in Chicago?

Love,
Noël

Dear Noël,

What in the world are you writing about, to want to know about my fur coat? There is a story.

When I worked in Chicago in the early 1940s, my cousin Camilla Kellar (Aunt Anne Hughes's daughter, sister of Phyllis) urged me to go to Appleton, Wisconsin, and buy a custom coat from furrier Eddie Myers. I took a train and put up in a small hotel overnight. (All night I could hear music from a bar somewhere across the street. It made me wonder if that was the setting in another Wisconsin town the winter night in 1898 when two Christian traveling salesmen met in a small hotel in Boscobel and shared evening devotions. On the spot they decided to do something to spread the gospel among other traveling men. Thus was born Gideons International, now in 175 countries.)

Oh, well, back to the fur coat. The coat came just in time for my first subzero experience. Snugly inside it, I was cozy and comfy, no matter the sharp winds off Lake Michigan a block or two away.

That's a lot of words to say—mink-dyed muskrat. That is probably all you really wanted to know, but memories go with lots of things.

I love you,
Mother

What Do I Do with This Heirloom?

It's been in our attic for three decades, the shabby orange-and-white corrugated wardrobe box we saved from the movers. For a few years we hung out-of-season clothes in it, but now it's packed with unwanted items left behind one by one when each new season blew in. If you were to wipe the dust from the lid and lift it away, you'd find one piece that's been there for all the thirty years—my mother's mink-dyed muskrat coat.

She didn't really need it anymore, living in warm Georgia. And she was worried about me in Minnesota's deep-freeze winters. The coat was already thirty years old and showing its age when she sent it to me. I tried it on and felt like a bear. And, besides, with all my friends wearing ponchos and pea coats, it seemed just "too too." I don't remember if I ever wore it.

But you can't just toss an icon. I knew its story. This coat was a symbol of Mother's career-girl days, of the Virginia girl's fling in the Windy City, of her independent years sandwiched between life with parents and life as a parent. So I stashed the heirloom in the attic box. I'd decide later what to do with it. Looks like I'll be leaving the decision to my children. As Mother says, "Memories go with lots of things."

What Would We Do Without This Heirloom?

On the first morning of my first visit with my future husband's family, I lifted the fork for my initial taste of breakfast cake.

"Wait." Johnny stopped me. "This is the way we eat it." He dunked his chunk of cake into a cup filled with milk. Then he raised it to his mouth and, with white drops rolling down his wrist, bit off a big soggy corner. He rolled his eyes to the ceiling and groaned, "Mmm, mmm! They don't serve us this in the college dining hall, Ma Mohn." His five-foot-tall grandmother, Erma Mohn, just smiled.

She smiled again when I asked her later for the recipe. "Recipe? You can watch and write down what I do." So I watched and wrote: "Four handfuls of flour, a walnut-sized lump of butter . . ." She told me that she learned breakfast cake from her mother, Geneva Stoner, and that she had learned it from her mother, Martha Loos—an heirloom recipe. Years later, when Ma Mohn died, I packed a frozen breakfast cake into my suitcase to take to the other grandchildren gathered for her funeral.

Our children have always expected breakfast cake on birthday and holiday mornings. As young adults, they ask for it when they're home for a visit. After Ma Mohn's death, I thought of myself as the chief guardian of this family keepsake,

Ma Mohn's Breakfast Cake

Mix together until the texture of meal:

2 c. flour	1 tsp. salt
1 c. sugar	1 tsp. baking powder
1 stick margarine, cut into 5-6 pieces	

Remove "handful" ($1/3$ to $1/2$ cup) of this mix and save for topping.

Mix together in large measuring cup or a bowl:

1 c. milk

1 Tbs. vinegar

1 tsp. baking soda

Add liquid mixture to dry mixture, along with

2 eggs

Mix well and pour into greased 9 x 13 cake pan or 10 x 15 jelly roll pan. Sprinkle with topping.

Topping

Mix together:

Reserved dry ingredients

1-2 tsp. cinnamon (optional)

$1/2$ c. flour	$1/2$ c. brown sugar

Lump of margarine the size of a large walnut (2-3 Tbs.)

Bake for 25-30 minutes at 325 degrees.

until we visited Benjamin and Melissa, our son and his bride, and she served us breakfast cake. So now this heirloom belongs also to my children, who are at least the sixth generation enjoying it.

Traditions are a lot like heirlooms. Both probably have come to us through our families. Some you love; you can't imagine life without them. Some you're stuck with; you don't know what to do with them.

What are the traditions we're leaving our children, the next generation? Which traditions deserve to be stuck away in the attic? Into which traditions do we love to draw other people?

GOD—OUR FATHER AND OUR INHERITANCE

Both heirlooms and good traditions strengthen our sense of history and belonging. As Christians, our history is God's story of drawing us into his family. "'I will be a father to you, and you shall be sons and daughters to me,' says the Lord Almighty" (2 Corinthians 6:18).

It is as God's children that we find our sense of belonging. "You have received the spirit of adoption as sons, by whom we cry, 'Abba! Father!' The Spirit himself bears witness with our spirit that we are children of God, and if children, then heirs—heirs of God and fellow heirs with Christ" (Romans 8:15-17).

We who are trusting Christ are the heirs of our Father, God. But what is the inheritance that we want from our Father? In this passage, Paul pictures us calling to him, "Abba! Father!" We are like children at the end of a long day. The only thing we want is our abba, our daddy. The yearning of our hearts is for him. And that is the great treasure we inherit from our heavenly Father—himself.

As David wrote in Psalm 37:4, "Delight yourself in the LORD, and he will give you the desires of your heart." The inheritance we will receive from God is what we delight in most gladly and desire most deeply, the Lord himself.

With any other father, we would not receive our inheritance until he died. But God is eternal; he never dies. He is the Father who never leaves us nor forsakes us (Hebrews 13:5). He gives us himself.

We might wonder what is left to inherit if we have already been adopted into his family and he's already our Father. What more is there to look forward to? The apostle John answers: "See what kind of love the Father has given to us, that we should be called children of God; and so we are. . . . Beloved, we are God's children now, and what we will be has not yet appeared; but we know that when he appears we shall be like him, because we shall see him as he is" (1 John 3:1-2).

He is our Father now, and we are his children now. Yet we are still waiting for something—to see him as he is, to be like him as we long to be, and to have the passion of God himself to enjoy him. That is our complete inheritance—the full enjoyment of God himself.

Although this book offers ideas that I hope will be helpful as examples of God-centered traditions, this is not a how-to manual. I am praying that it will inspire us to look at God with fresh eyes, to see and love and desire the treasure that he is. And I'm praying that the traditions of our lives will be filled with the treasure that fills our heart on "everyday" days and on "especially" days.

WHY DO TRADITIONS MATTER?

My husband and I moved into marriage with traditions we inherited from our parents. Having come of age in the '60s though, breathing the air of anti-authority, no one was going to tell us we had to do everything just like Mom and Dad! But we did love our parents, and we loved God and wanted our family life to reflect that. So to this day, we've kept many "hand-me-downs" from our parents—daily family Bible reading and prayer, for example.

Our first conscious challenge to think seriously about what role traditions would play in our own family came—as it does for many people—with the birth of our first child. The moment we set foot into our apartment with our newborn, panic poured over me. We had walked out this door as two, I realized, and now we were walking in as three—forever there would be one more of us. We were responsible for this life, and I couldn't even keep a philodendron healthy!

By God's grace, our son lived and thrived. My first panic ebbed, replaced by tides of deeper responsibilities. The instant a raindrop falls into the sea, you can't make it separate again. When God entrusted a child to us, in an instant that baby became so intimately a part of us that we couldn't picture life without him—ever. I couldn't imagine what my chubby child would be when he grew up. But what I yearned for had little to do with his adult career. I longed that he be part of us forever—that he be God's forever.

That aspiration blew away any contentment we might have had in assumptions that we'd just keep on doing things the way we'd always done. Now we had to think, not just act out of habit.

"WHY?"—THE BIG QUESTION

In early December, for instance, when Karsten was just over a year old, I thought about our meager Christmas traditions. I tried to see them through the eyes of a curious toddler. I imagined the conversations he and I might have during the month:

"Huzz-at?"

"Candles."

Then I mentally supplied the question he wouldn't even know yet to ask: "Why candles?"

"Why?" I realized that was a question I was going to have to answer from now on, not just for Christmas traditions that particular year, but for all years and every day. At that moment I knew that "just because" was no answer. Nor was "because that's the way Grandmother and Granddaddy do it" or "because it's pretty" or "because it's convenient" or "because that's what everybody does."

In the book of Exodus, Moses displays his understanding of the nature of children and the responsibility of parents: "And when your children say to you, 'What do you mean by this service?' you shall say, 'It is the sacrifice of the LORD's Passover, for he passed over the houses of the people of Israel in Egypt'" (12:26-27).

Moses assumes children will ask why. And he instructs parents to give an answer that speaks of reality. This instruction is all in the context of laying out for children ceremonies that will portray the answer. He is giving them the answer, both spoken and displayed. And the answer is God—God saved us, and we honor him, worship him, thank him. We and our children need this kind of yearly repetition to impress us with the weight of what God has done.

Traditions are important for another reason. We've already seen one huge difference between the inheritance we receive from God and the one we receive from our physical families: God is both our Father and our present and future inheritance, our heirloom.

ONLY GOD CAN BEQUEATH GOD

There's another big difference between this inheritance and any other that we might receive: You can't bequeath God to your children. You can leave them the fur coat from your mother, the forested acres from your father, the carved cane from Uncle Claude, and the clock from your grandmother, but they can't inherit God from you. God can only be inherited from God.

BARNABAS'S BAPTISM

When Jesus calls a boy to live
He bids him come and die,
And promises that he will give
The Spirit in reply.

He bids him turn from deadly sin
And trust a dying Christ,
And find that he will live again
Beyond the sacrifice.

He bids him bury doubt and dread
Beneath the water here
And raises him then from the dead
And leaves the drowning fear.

He robes the boy with righteousness
And covers crimson wrong,
And furnishes with royal dress
And makes his spirit strong.

So I rejoice to stand with you,
My son, within the grave
That you and I are passing through;
Where God alone can save.

Eleven years I've called you son,
And that is dearly true,
And now because of what God's done
I call you brother too.

JOHN PIPER, JUNE 5, 1994

That's what my mother was saying one night when I was six. As she kissed me good night and tucked me in, she said, "Now that you're trusting Jesus as your Savior, I'm your mother and your sister." She was acknowledging the words of Galatians 3:26: "In Christ Jesus you are all sons of God, through faith." We only become God's children through our faith, not through our parents' faith. I had gained a relationship with God in the same way she had. We both had become his daughters by adoption, through faith. I was not God's granddaughter who inherited God through my mother's relationship with him. I was God's daughter who inherited God directly from God.

To all who did receive him, who believed in his name, he gave the right to become children of God. (JOHN 1:12)

Now although we cannot bequeath God to our children, we can help them know him and understand him in ways that prepare them to believe in his name. "Everyday" and "especially" traditions in a family are an important part of that teaching, of picturing who God is and what he's done in our home and in the world. Traditions are a vital way of displaying our greatest treasure, of showing what—Who—is most important to us.

We need to remember, too, that when our traditions are displaying the Treasure of our lives, he is there to be seen by everyone who comes within our circle. Jesus said, "Let your light shine before others, so that they may see your good works and give glory to your Father who is in heaven" (Matthew 5:16). God wants our family and others to give glory to him because they've seen his light through us. Paul says we should be "children of God without blemish in the midst of a crooked and twisted generation, among whom you shine as lights in the world, holding fast to the word of life" (Philippians 2:15-16).

GUIDING QUESTIONS FOR ALL OUR TRADITIONS ALL YEAR

• What is my greatest treasure? What is most precious to me?
• How do I reflect and express that treasure in my life?
• How can I pass that treasure on to my children
and others within my circle?

TWO

WHAT IS
TRADITION?

Habits, Customs, Traditions— What's the Difference?

If we brush our teeth three times a day, we don't call that a tradition. We call it a habit. But when we pray before each meal every day—giving thanks to God who feeds us—we might call it a habit, and we might also call it a tradition.

Every time I drive home with a trunk full of groceries, I honk "Shave and a haircut, two bits!" to signal my husband or one of my sons to come out and haul the bags into the kitchen. (The dog goes bananas even if the boys don't.) That's one of our family's customs, but we don't call it a tradition.

On Thanksgiving and other special holidays, the rule at our house is: If the women fix it, the men clean it up. (Guess who created that rule! Well, I had good reason. For twenty-two years I was the only woman in our kitchen!) After the males have done their mealtime share of licking the platter clean, they form a relay team clearing the table, scraping dishes, washing, drying, and putting away. Never mind that it takes me a week to find everything again—it's worth it. That's their gift to me so that I can emerge from the kitchen and enjoy the special day with them. It's a tradition I'm passing on to my daughters-in-law and daughter.

People have many habits or customs, such as taking off shoes when entering a house, that we wouldn't call traditions. On the other hand, good traditions become so woven into our lives that they are also habits or customs.

What Makes Something a Tradition?

Every good gift, including traditions, comes to us "from above, coming down from the Father of lights" (James 1:17). God is the inventor of tradition, just as he is the inventor and giver of every other good gift. We could wish for no better authority to answer our question: What makes something a tradition? So let's think about some of the times when God was creating traditions for his people.

The word *tradition* isn't in the Old Testament, but the reality is there. In the passages where God gives instructions for the ceremonies he designed, he repeatedly makes clear his purposes for these occasions. When we recognize his purposes, we'll have a better idea as to what makes a godly tradition in our own homes. About the Passover celebration, for example, we read:

> It was a night of watching by the LORD, to bring them out of the land of Egypt; so this same night is a night of watching kept to the LORD by all the people of Israel throughout their generations. (Exodus 12:42)

Some of the phrases in the verse help us see at least some of what God had intended for his people through their traditions.

- *"A night of watching by the LORD"*—God wants his people to remember what he himself did for them.

- *"A night . . . to the LORD"*—God wants them to honor him for what he's done.

- *"Throughout their generations"*—God wants their children and grandchildren and great-grandchildren to hear the story of his salvation so they too will remember and honor him.

If we look at God's instructions for the Festival of Booths commemorating the Jews' forty years of desert wanderings, we see another important piece of his purpose.

- *You shall dwell in booths for seven days. All native Israelites shall dwell in booths, that your generations may know that I made the people of Israel dwell in booths when I brought them out of the land of Egypt:* I am the LORD your God. (Leviticus 23:42-43, emphasis added)

As with the Passover, God wants his people to celebrate in a way that re-enacts the story of his mighty deeds. And again he wants the coming generations to hear the story and celebrate him and what he's done. Then there is an additional piece:

- *"I am the LORD your God"*—God was not just part of their history. Their traditions are to proclaim that he is their God now. He is I AM.

TRADITIONS—FOR WHOM?

Recently I waited in line at the information desk of a book supermarket. But when my turn came and I asked what they had on traditions, the answer man had no answers, just questions: "You mean like for African-Americans or Native Americans?" Apparently, to him tradition implied ethnic. Then I drove to a nearby Christian bookstore and asked the same question. "You mean like for kids?" But there was nothing in stock anyway.

So who are our traditions for? Let's go back to the Creator of tradition. Yes, God gave the adults instructions for the Passover and other rituals. But was it all just for the sake of the children? Was it mainly to give the adults ways to make sure the kids knew their history? In Deuteronomy 11 Moses had some other words for those same adults.

TRADITIONS—NOT JUST FOR THE CHILDREN'S SAKE

Yes, this passage does end with children. But first come some strong words to the adults. Moses points directly to them: "You shall therefore love the LORD your God" (v. 1). And in case they didn't get the point, he spells it out in verse 2: "I am not speaking to your children who have not known or seen it."

DEUTERONOMY 11:1-3, 7, 18-19

¹You shall therefore love the LORD your God and keep his charge, his statutes, his rules, and his commandments always. ²And consider today (since I am not speaking to your children who have not known or seen it), consider the discipline of the LORD your God, his greatness, his mighty hand and his outstretched arm, ³his signs and his deeds that he did. . . . ⁷For your eyes have seen all the great work of the LORD that he did. . . . ¹⁸You shall therefore lay up these words of mine in your heart and in your soul, and you shall bind them as a sign on your hand, and they shall be as frontlets between your eyes. ¹⁹You shall teach them to your children, talking of them when you are sitting in your house, and when you are walking by the way, and when you lie down, and when you rise. (See also Deuteronomy 6.)

Grownups are the ones who have a history with God. We have leaned on his strength, learned his love, and depended on his faithfulness. We have suffered the pain of his discipline and felt the relief of his forgiveness. Our youngest children don't understand much yet about these things. They will learn from their experiences as they grow older and from the Christian adults in their lives.

PEOPLE WITH NO CHILDREN

Which adults are responsible to display the Lord to the children? Moses doesn't separate young parents from the rest. He's speaking to *all* the adults. This means that tradition is important for all of us, even if there are no children in our lives. But most of us do have some children in our circles, even if they're not in our immediate household. We have grandchildren, nieces, nephews, or Sunday school kids. Once more, before he talks about the children, Moses stresses the responsibility of all the adults: "Lay up these words of mine in *your* heart and in *your* soul" (verse 18, emphasis mine).

If you are single, traditions may be even more important for you. Your traditions may involve peers who are friends, other adults you want to minister to, and the children in your life—neighbors, students, friends' children. The traditions you develop and practice will draw others into being your family circle. They can play an important role in keeping you from being isolated.

The apostle Paul is a good illustration of a single man who took seriously his responsibility to a younger person in his life. As far as we can tell, Timothy's father was not a spiritual influence in his life. But when Timothy was a young man, Paul became a fatherly friend. He wrote Timothy about the importance of following a godly example, spelling out the very qualities we want to see developed in children through our teaching and tradition.

You, however, have followed my teaching, my conduct, my aim in life, my faith, my patience, my love, my steadfastness, my persecutions and sufferings. . . . Indeed, all who desire to live a godly life in Christ Jesus will be persecuted. . . . But as for you, continue in what you have learned and have firmly believed, knowing from whom you learned it. (2 TIMOTHY 3:10-14)

"Knowing from whom you learned it." If we are loving the Lord and storing his Word in our hearts and souls and keeping our souls diligently, we will be people who, with God helping us, can say, "Continue in what you have learned . . . knowing from whom you learned it." In his relationship with young Timothy, Paul was following the example of Moses—laying up in his own heart and soul the Lord's words and then teaching them.

We can only give what we already have. If God's words are not in our own hearts and souls, we can't teach them to anyone else. If we don't love God ourselves, we can't live out his love for others to see and experience.

"BUT I'M SO IMPERFECT!"

Of course, our love for God is never perfect, and we won't know him and his Word completely until we see him face to face (1 Corinthians 13:12). But isn't Deuteronomy 11:18 encouraging? It doesn't say we need to have all of God's Word down pat before we're ready to teach. It says, "Lay up these words of mine in your heart and in your soul." For the rest of our lives, with God's help, we will keep on making God's Word our own, making it more and more the beat of our heart and the breath of our soul.

LETTER FROM A
SINGLE FRIEND

Dear Noël:
Even though they were not Christian traditions (because none of us were Christians when I was growing up), traditions were an important part of my heritage. Grandpa always came for Christmas dinner. Christmas was a time when my father agreed not to drink, although he sometimes failed to live up to his promise. We always had turkey and dressing and both pumpkin and mincemeat pie, as only my mom could make. We never got many gifts, but early on we learned to give as well as to receive. I can remember going to the Ben Franklin store and poring over all the merchandise, trying to come up with a gift for my mom. I finally decided on a package of Wrigley's gum, her favorite.

It was difficult for many years to make myself fit into the traditions of other families, thinking that they were just that—family traditions. But now I love being invited to people's homes on special occasions and being a part of their special traditions.

The only thing I might add to your thoughts regarding singles is the command from Psalm 78 to "tell the next generation the praises of the Lord." I've always taken that as my mandate. Perhaps just as married people need to make their own traditions as well as incorporate those they've learned as children, singles need to make their own traditions after they leave the nest, traditions that will carry on in someone's life after they're gone.

The rest of verse 18 is God's method for laying up his words: "You shall bind them as a sign on your hand, and they shall be as frontlets between your eyes." Moses may have had something literal in mind here for the Jews. But even so, there was a practical godly purpose behind these instructions—to help his people live and breathe and move in the air of God's Word. That practical godly goal is ours, too. We should keep God's Word as available and as visible as if it were hanging between our eyes—as if everything we see and do comes through his filter. His Word should be as if it were tied on our hands so that all our acts are directed and shaped by his Word.

And with that as our quest, we move into the next part of God's pattern for teaching and tradition.

Traditions Are Also for the Children

You shall teach [God's words] to your children, talking of them when you are sitting in your house, and when you are walking by the way, and when you lie down, and when you rise. (Deuteronomy 11:19)

When I get caught up in the biography of a person I admire, my family hears all about this person for days. Whatever someone says seems to remind me of some event in her life. So mealtime conversations are filled with stories that flow from my own fascination. As we are filling our hearts and souls with God's Word, what will be more natural than the same sort of spillover onto our family?

But are we really talking about tradition here? Isn't this passage about teaching and about God's Word? Yes, and one of the main features of traditions is repetition. Of course, we wouldn't say that sitting or walking or lying down or rising up, no matter how frequently they're repeated, are traditions. But those activities represent the things that we do most often, and they are named as reminders to do the most crucial thing we can do for our children—teach them the words of God. God wants us to remember to see him in the most mundane parts of our lives. And what we see, he wants us to talk about with our children. When that level of significance is added to the ordinary repetitions of life, a tradition is created.

Sitting, walking, lying down, and rising up are so insignificant that we don't even give them a thought. But I pray that my children will look back at "insignificant" times and ask each other, "Remember trying to catch Mom and Dad before they got up in the morning so we could snuggle with them, and how lots of times Daddy prayed out loud before we all got out of bed?" or

"Remember when we asked questions, and somehow the answers always came back to God?"

Things like that don't just happen. They come first from our own hearts that are tuned in to God. Then they happen because we *plan* to include our children in the God-air we breathe. Without planning, we'll practice our Bible memory just once or twice and then no more. We'll do lots of good things, but only a couple of times. One of the great strengths of good traditions in our lives is the *repetition*— not something done once, then something else, then another thing altogether, but good things done regularly, dependably, until they become habits.

There are two kinds of traditions—"everyday" and "especially." Deuteronomy 11:18 is speaking of the everyday kind. A little later we'll think some more about this sort and also about the "especially" traditions, the kind that come only every year, such as holidays or birthdays, or even less frequently.

The Essence of Tradition

We've seen in Deuteronomy 11 the essence, the core, of tradition for God's people: "You shall therefore lay up these words of mine in your heart and in your soul" (v. 18). The things we do regularly that help us in our deepest being to know and love and want God, the things that help our lives to be infiltrated with God—those things are tradition. And then if there are children in our lives, to pass these God-focused activities to the next generation—that's what tradition is for a Christian.

Deuteronomy 4:9-10 is a good summary of what we've seen so far—our responsibility as adults to stay close to God, to remember his work in our lives, and to tell the children about it so that we and they will fear and honor the Lord. Moses said to the people:

> Only take care, and keep your soul diligently, lest you forget the things that your eyes have seen, and lest they depart from your heart all the days of your life. Make them known to your children and your children's children—how on the day that you stood before the LORD your God . . . the LORD said to me, "Gather the people to me, that I may let them hear my words, so that they may learn to fear me all the days that they live on the earth, and that they may teach their children so."

From these Deuteronomy passages, we can cull at least three ways of defining tradition:

- Definition 1: A tradition is a planned habit with significance.
- Definition 2: Tradition is the handing down of
  > information,
  > beliefs,
  > worldview
  >> from one generation to another
  >> by word of mouth
  >> and by regular repetition
  >>> of example
  >>> of ceremony
  >>> of celebration.
- Definition 3: For a Christian,
  > tradition is laying up God's words
  > in our own hearts
  > and passing his words
  >> to the next generation.

Definitions are important as skeletons,
but we can't live with just bones. In the remaining chapters,
we'll cover these bones with some flesh:
- What information?
- Which beliefs?
- What sort of worldview?

THREE

WHAT MAKES
TRADITION
IMPORTANT?

T hrough a Milky Way of lightning bugs, my cousins and I darted from pine trunk to persimmon tree, hiding from each other. By now we'd forgotten who was It. Our silent thrills came from bumping into *anyone* in the true dark of a Georgia country summer night. *Silent* thrills because if we didn't remind our parents of our presence, they'd talk till midnight over there on Uncle Buddy and Aunt Lou Ellen's familiar unpainted farmhouse front porch—the house where Granddaddy and Grandmother Henry had raised Daddy and Uncle Buddy and all the rest. The house where Grandmother had taught her children her favorite Scripture passage:

> *My sheep hear my voice, and I know them, and they follow me: And I give unto them eternal life; and they shall never perish, neither shall any man pluck them out of my hand. My Father, which gave them me, is greater than all; and no man is able to pluck them out of my Father's hand. I and my Father are one.*
>
> (JOHN 10:27-30 KJV)

It was a tradition that we children could take turns spending the night with Grandmother. As with all good traditions, we knew what to expect. She would make sure that each of us learned those words of John proclaiming the deity of Jesus and the sweetness and the power of his voice.

By the time I grew up and the farmhouse had long since been crushed into the red dust by a kudzu jungle, my sixteen aunts and uncles and gazillion cousins (I guess Grandmother knew the exact number) were such a fixture in my life that I could almost forget they were there. I took them for granted, like the roots of a tree. If asked, you'd know a tree depends on a wide, deep network of roots, but do you think of that support when you're enjoying the shade of a giant oak?

That oblivion toward the roots of my family tree changed for me in March a few years ago. As azaleas and dogwoods painted Georgia's springtime pine woods, I arrived with my children to watch as Daddy faded and died. Less than an hour after he was gone, Aunt Lou Ellen arrived from her home half an hour away and was washing dishes at Mother's sink. Uncle Buddy wasn't with her now because he had been the first of the brothers and sisters to die. By the next day the uncles and aunts had arrived from Louisiana, South Carolina, and Tennessee, and cousins were pouring in from even farther away.

I stood in the midst of the hubbub with Aunt Lou Ellen, the first widow of that generation in our family. When I talked, she listened, grasping both my hands. When I cried, her eyes flooded over, too. When she hugged me, it seemed as if her feelings flashed through my nerves.

That night at the funeral home, after the town had visited and gone home, my brothers and sisters and I sat in a circle across the room from the casket where our father lay. We had things to talk about—some simply practical and others more difficult. When I heard hymns from another room, I assumed at first it was a custodian's boom box. But soon I realized that we weren't the only late-night group still there. Our uncles and aunts had made their own circle to pray for us and to worship our Lord, the one who gives and who takes away (Job 1:21).

The days surrounding Daddy's funeral reawakened me to my extended family. I still live far away from them. I still don't think of them every day. But when I do, it's with a firm sense of their place in my life and of mine in theirs. They showed me that they're there when I need them. Their example has encouraged me to be like them—many parts, yet one body caring for one another, suffering or rejoicing together as the body of Christ (1 Corinthians 12:20-25).

"My sheep hear my voice. . . ." Those words are a symbol of the traditions that send my mind back to grandparents, parents, uncles, and aunts who are like roots through which God has given me life and strength.

TRADITIONS LOOK FORWARD

God used my family to lead me to love and trust him. When I moved away from my parents' home, though, I soon realized that not everyone can look back to a family that supported them and pointed them toward God. But the Good Shepherd does not limit his sheep to only those from good families.

IN MEMORY OF
DR. GEORGE HENRY
*Reflections on Psalm 1
and Joshua 24:15*

No tree however deep the roots,
However high and green the shoots,
However strong the trunk has stood,
Or firm the fibers of the wood,
No tree was ever meant to be
A never-ending shade for me
Or you. Save one: where Jesus died
With bleeding branches spread as wide
And far as faith for sinful men.

But there was shade, especially when
The tree was old: the leaves were thick
With life, and though the root was sick,
The bark deep-creased with age, the limbs
Were laden down with love, and hymns
Were heard beneath when wind bestirred
The bowing branches with the Word
Of heav'n. O there were years of shade!

And more: there was the fruit he made,
Or better, bore, when all the ground
Seemed dry, we turned again and found
The branches heavy with some rare
Well-watered food and sweet called Care.
There must have been a river there
Beneath the arid earth somewhere
Deep-flowing up around the tips
Of dying roots, and giving sips
Of everlasting life for him
To share with us while every limb
Gave up its own. O, there was fruit!
Life-giving from the dying root.

And more. Much more. There was
   the wood,
And it was strong. It had withstood
A thousand storms, and every one
More firm. And now for every son,
Grandchild and every daughter here
He lies a fallen tree and dear,
And leaves in you the solid wood
And bids you stand where he has stood
Beside the river of the Word,
And that you keep what you have heard,
And sing with him in one accord:
"My fruitful house will serve the Lord."

JOHN PIPER (MARCH 1992)

In 2 Chronicles, for example, Josiah became king of Judah when he was eight, following Manasseh, his grandfather, who "led Judah and the inhabitants of Jerusalem astray," (33:9) and Amon, his father, who "did what was evil in the sight of the LORD" (33:22). In spite of this wicked heritage and his youthfulness, Josiah "did what was right in the eyes of the LORD. . . . For in the eighth year of his reign, while he was yet a boy, he began to seek the God of David" (34:2-3).

Before there ever was a family, there was God. He is not weakened or changed by the failure of a family. When we are God's, we look back and realize that we were dependent on him for everything even before we knew him. As grateful as I am for my family, they were not the ones who saved me. I am dependent wholly on God. In that most ultimate regard, we believers are all the same, no matter what our background.

In Psalm 71 the psalmist reminds us that our reliance upon God began even before birth, even before our family began to have any influence on us for either good or evil. A public health nurse whose job is to assist people in crisis told me, "I deal with so many people whose lives have been terrible. You wonder what hope there is. This is so helpful, realizing that God knew us and was working for us even before we were born and affected by our family."

And our relationship with him lasts beyond death. If Psalm 71:9 were a question, we'd call it rhetorical—a question whose answer is so obvious that it becomes a statement. So when the psalmist prays that God not forsake him when he is old, we hear him thinking of the future when God will be as dependable as ever, as worthy as ever of praise, as glorious as ever. He will be the same God at the end of life as he was at the beginning. And no one can pluck his own from his hand, ever.

Even if our background is not good, it is *back*ground, behind us. What is ahead? How can we make family and life different for the household that God has given us now? The psalmist's description of his interaction with God is what we want for ourselves and our children: "My mouth is filled with your praise, and with your glory all the day" (v. 8). That's what we want to embody in our traditions so that we see and praise God.

When I look toward my children and their children, I am strongly aware of my responsibility to the family that comes after me. From their births, I have always wanted my children to know as much about God as they were

PSALM 71:6-9

6Upon you I have leaned from before my birth;
you are he who took me from my mother's womb.
My praise is continually of you.
7I have been as a portent to many,
but you are my strong refuge.
8My mouth is filled with your praise,
and with your glory all the day.
9Do not cast me off in the time of old age;
forsake me not when my strength is spent.

able to grasp at whatever age they were. And I have wanted my life and our family to be a picture of God to others—that we be the body of Christ who presents an image of Christ to the people around us.

WE STAND IN THE MIDDLE

While I am still daughter, niece, cousin, and sister, now I am also aunt, mother, grandmother, and friend. I am a basketball player at the center circle, catching the ball passed from the backcourt and pivoting to advance it down court.

In Psalm 78 the psalmist was also looking both backward and forward. Try to count the generations he names.

1. *Our parents* ("our fathers"—verse 3)

2. *Our own generation* ("their children"—verse 4)

3. *Our children* ("the next generation"—verse 4)

4. *A generation who lived many years before our parents* ("Our fathers," verse 5, seems to imply the ancestors who received the law during Moses' time, which was centuries before this psalm was written.)

> PSALM 78:1-7
>
> [1]Give ear, O my people, to my teaching;
> incline your ears to the words of my mouth!
> [2]I will open my mouth in a parable;
> I will utter dark sayings from of old,
> [3]things that we have heard and known,
> that our fathers have told us.
> [4]We will not hide them from their children,
> but tell to the coming generation
> the glorious deeds of the LORD, and his might,
> and the wonders that he has done.
> [5]He established a testimony in Jacob
> and appointed a law in Israel,
> which he commanded our fathers
> to teach to their children,
> [6]that the next generation might know them,
> the children yet unborn,
> and arise and tell them to their children,
> [7]so that they should set their hope in God
> and not forget the works of God,
> but keep his commandments.

5. *All the generations between those ancient ancestors and our own parents* ("their children"—verse 5)

6. *Our grandchildren* ("the children yet unborn"—verse 6)

7. *Our great-grandchildren* ("their children"—verse 6)

It's easy to see, though, that the writer is not giving us a specific generation count. What he's doing is looking so far backward and so far into the future that we know he means all generations of those who follow the God of Abraham. Of course, we don't know exactly how many generations have come before us, and we don't know how many generations will be born in the future. That's not the point. Here's the psalmist's point: Beginning with God's call of Abraham—the time when there began to be a particular people called "God's people"—God commanded adults to teach the children. We are part of a millennia-long line, with the same command and responsibility to teach our children that the first generation had.

What are we to teach them?

1. *The glorious deeds of the Lord* (verse 4)—what God has done in our lives.

2. *The might of God* (verse 4)—the nature of God.

3. *The wonders God has done* (verse 4)—what God has done in history.

4. *The testimony and law of God* (verse 5)—how God wants us to live.

These areas of instruction are a confirmation and repetition of the guidelines the people of God received in Deuteronomy 11 where Moses charged the Israelites to teach the children about God's greatness and might, his signs and deeds, and his words and commandments.

> I have always wanted my children to know as much about God as they were able to grasp at whatever age they were.
>   And
>   I have wanted my life and our family to be a picture of God to others—
>   that we be the body of Christ who presents an image of Christ to the people around us.

We might ask again what the relationship is between tradition and what we teach. It is this: The heart is the same. For a Christian, the heart of our traditions, and the heart of our teaching is God, whom we know through his acts and his words.

Now look at the reasons the psalmist gives us for our traditions (verse 7):

1. *That they* [our children and grandchildren and great- . . .] *should set their hope in God*—our deepest desire for our children and their children,

2. *and not forget the works of God*—the basis of their trust,

3. *but keep his commandments*—the life they will live because of their trust in God.

Traditions are memories, and they are for memory. Our children and grandchildren don't have to be locked into the small world of their own experience with God. Traditions give them a whole world's worth and a whole history's worth of God.

"That they should set their hope in God and not forget the works of God, but keep his commandments. . ."

We will not be here forever for our children, but God will.

FOUR

HOW DO
TRADITIONS
TEACH?

Karsten and Benjamin snuggled under their quilts, turning up their cheeks for good night kisses from their daddy. When he started singing, *"Wer nur den lieben Gott laesst walten,"* a favorite hymn he'd memorized when we lived in Germany, ten-year-old Karsten sat up suddenly. "What was that red light that used to shine when you sang that song?"

Red light? At first we had no idea what he meant. But there was only one possibility, as unlikely as it seemed. Nine years earlier we had worn a path along the long, dark hallway in our German apartment, trying to help baby Karsten sleep. During miles of pacing, Karsten's daddy had soothed him with, *"Wer nur den lieben Gott laesst walten."* At one end of the hall was the kitchen door. At the other was the bathroom door with a marble-sized *red light* over it that glowed when the bathroom heater was on. When we left that apartment and Germany, Karsten was still too young to talk.

Do you think we'd been training him all the years since to remember that red light? No. Once we walked out the door the final time, we'd never given it another thought. But Karsten had stared over his daddy's shoulder at that red glow each lap of the route they'd plodded together—who knows how many hundreds of repetitions? And each time, he'd heard, *"Wer nur den lieben Gott laesst walten."* Repetition had installed the red light securely in his mind. The sound of the hymn switched on the light in his memory.

We are always teaching our children, whether we mean to or not. Our children come to believe, probably unconsciously, that whatever is repeated regularly has significance. It was God's design that learning happen by frequent and regular repetition. That kind of learning was part of what he had in mind when he told his people to teach the children his words, "talking of them when you are sitting in your house, and when you are walking by the way, and when you lie down, and when you rise" (Deuteronomy 11:19)—note how frequently and regularly.

One indication of God's wisdom in this command is that when our activities are filled with God, we have to be thinking about God; so our normal activities are helping us fulfill

Wer nur den lieben Gott laesst walten
Und hoffet auf ihn allezeit,
Den wird er wunderbar erhalten
In aller Not und Traurigkeit.
Wer Gott, dem Allerhoechsten, traut,
Der hat auf keinen Sand gebaut.

GEORG NEUMARK, 1657

If thou but suffer God to guide thee
And hope in Him through all thy ways,
He'll give thee strength, whate'er betide thee,
And bear thee through the evil days.
Who trusts in God's unchanging love
Builds on the rock that naught can move.

TRANSLATED BY CATHERINE WINKWORTH, 1863

God's command to "lay up these words of mine in your heart and in your soul" (Deuteronomy 11:18). Another sign of God's wisdom is that, with enough repetition, the very activities, no matter how mundane they are, will trigger thoughts of God in our minds, just as the hymn triggered the memory of a red light in Karsten's mind.

PLANNING

In order to "teach [God's words] to your children, talking of them when you are sitting in your house, and when you are walking by the way, and when you lie down, and when you rise" (Deuteronomy 11:19), you have to be *planning*—planning what to say and where, how, and when to say it. For me, not planning means my children receive a burst of God-talk for a day or two. Then when that particular gush of affection dies down, we're back to just taking God for granted, rather than talking about him and recognizing him in all the parts of our day. That's not what I want to teach my children—that God is experienced in a random pattern of a few days of enthusiasm followed by days of silence. One of the things Deuteronomy 11:19 makes clear is that God doesn't like being taken for granted. Rather, he wants to be talked about a lot.

All of us are training our children both intentionally and unintentionally. We need to make sure we aren't leaving the important things to happenstance. We know it's crucial that they become familiar with God, our Heirloom and our only hope for real life. We yearn for them to love and trust and follow Christ. It would be foolish just to wait for them to learn that by chance. We must *plan* to reflect God and teach about Christ in the repeated events of our lives.

GOD'S GLUE

The repeated God-oriented events in our lives are like God's glue. I saw that in my own family as I was growing up. It's amazing my parents stayed together. I know that now. About twenty years into their marriage, their rampaging differences seemed about to rip them apart.

God does not like to be taken for granted. It flies in the face of his eternal purposes--that he be known and loved and praised and enjoyed.

And it makes us superficial people. . . . When the main thing is missing, what's left is distorted and superficial, whatever it is.

If someone says, "Oh, that's just religion. You can't expect everything to be religion," I answer, "It's *not* religion. It's reality. God made the world and everything in it. He owns the earth and everyone on it. He is the main actor in the world. He is guiding the history of every people and nation to their appointed goals. Everything, without exception, has to do with God and gets its main meaning from God. And not to show this, but to take this for granted, is to be superficial. . . ."

It is simply impossible to overstate the importance of God.

And he does not like being taken for granted. The psalm does not say, "Great is the LORD, and greatly to be taken for granted." It says, "Great is the LORD, and greatly to be praised" (Psalm 96:4).

JOHN PIPER
"GOD IS A VERY IMPORTANT PERSON"[1]

God used his divine double-ingredient epoxy to hold them together. From one tube came their determination to make it. I never heard the word *divorce* from them, and it never occurred to me as a possibility. Then to create an even stronger bond, God stirred in the contents of the second tube—faithful family devotional habits.

Through even the most difficult months—years really—Daddy and Mother took us all to church every Sunday. There was never any question; it was simply a regular part of each week. And every evening of the week, one of us kids was sent to the front porch to holler down toward the pasture and out toward the woods, "sto-o-ory and pra-a-yers ti-i-ime!" After all nine of us (later we were ten) had tumbled into the living room from the barn and creek and kitchen, Daddy read the next passage in our years-long path through the whole Bible. Then we kneeled at our chairs and took turns praying. Or if it was a late night, we said the Lord's Prayer together.

I realize now how difficult that must have been for my parents. Often they must have felt like hypocrites, going through the motions when they didn't feel like worshiping or praying together. Of course, it would have been ideal if they had come before God with whole and happy hearts. But it was better to come somehow than not at all. And God held them together until he brought their marriage through the tempest into peace, using his glue of faithfulness—his faithfulness to them and their faithfulness to each other and to those family devotional traditions.

During that time we children were learning on two levels. One was unspoken but obvious: It is good and right for the family to worship together at church and at home. The other level was much deeper and became mortar in the foundation of our lives. We saw in the faithfulness of our parents a reflection, an image, of the faithfulness of God.

Perhaps that is the greatest value of good traditions. Through them we learn about and recognize and experience the faithfulness of our God, who promises, "I will not leave you or forsake you" (Joshua 1:5).

CONSISTENCY

"If a bullfrog had wings, he wouldn't bump his backside so much." That was always Daddy's response to my "what if" fantasies. I knew that what he meant was: "God made a bullfrog without wings, so he intended the old leaper to live with the bumps that jar his life. Same with you." Whenever I went to Mother with my worried imaginations, she said, "Sufficient unto the day is the evil thereof" (Matthew 6:34 KJV). Her sources might have been more refined, but her message was the same as Daddy's: "God is in control. Everything that comes to you is from him. And every thing that comes from him is good, even if it doesn't seem like it at the time."

Why do I remember these answers? Because I heard them consistently for a long time. What are some of the things you remember most clearly from your childhood? I'm guessing that many of them are events or words repeated frequently and regularly through many years.

We don't know exactly what our children's strongest, lasting memories will be. But we do want to make sure that our daily, weekly, "regularly random" activities occur in a God-filled context—that we recognize him in all of our life and show him everywhere to our children.

We can see from Psalm 71 that the psalmist thought this recognition of God was an everyday affair. Look at the plans he has in Psalm 71 to hope *continually*, to praise God *more and more* (v. 14), to tell of his righteousness and salvation *all the day* (v. 15), and to *still* proclaim his deeds (v. 17). We can see that his regular and consistent repetition of the praises of God are more than a possible plan; they are what he *intends* to do, what he is, in fact, already doing in the very act of proclaiming his intentions! His purpose is to broadcast the glories and wonders of God, to teach the next generation to know God.

Alongside that intentionality, there is also the unintentional aspect of teaching. When God is part of our everyday conversation and habits and life, we realize that while we are teaching particular things with our words, we are also teaching by our lives things that can't easily be put into words. The specific "truth jewels" we lay in our children's hands will, we pray, be stored in their heart's treasure chests; and the gems will be protectively surrounded by packing material, the wad of impressions, feelings, and assumptions they've picked up, both consciously and

PSALM 71:6-9, 14-19

⁶Upon you I have leaned from before my birth;
you are he who took me from my mother's womb.
My praise is continually of you.
⁷I have been as a portent to many,
but you are my strong refuge.
⁸My mouth is filled with your praise,
and with your glory all the day.
⁹Do not cast me off in the time of old age;
forsake me not when my strength is spent. ...
¹⁴I will hope continually
and will praise you yet more and more.
¹⁵My mouth will tell of your righteous acts,
of your deeds of salvation all the day,
for their number is past my knowledge.
¹⁶With the mighty deeds of the Lord GOD I will
come;
I will remind them of your righteousness, yours alone.
¹⁷O God, from my youth you have taught me,
and I still proclaim your wondrous deeds.
¹⁸So even to old age and gray hairs,
O God, do not forsake me,
until I proclaim your might to another generation,
your power to all those to come.
¹⁹Your righteousness, O God, reaches the high heavens.
You who have done great things,
O God, who is like you?

unconsciously, of who God is and what it means to be a family.

The factory for that packing material is our everyday lives. Our "everyday" traditions are the purposeful, significant activities that we do most frequently and regularly, the things that give shape to a day and a week. What are we teaching our children, both intentionally and unintentionally, during our "everyday" times? When Daddy says, "Let's pray," at every mealtime and, "Time for devotions" before every bedtime, he's not presenting a formal lesson. But he's packing his children's hearts with unspoken understandings about life—about how a husband leads, for example, and about the presence of God with us to hear our prayers and to speak to us through his Word.

That takes us back to the questions at the end of chapter 1, and we realize that it's not sufficient just to ask them about our traditions. We must ask them about the way we are living our lives.

- What is my greatest treasure? What is most precious to me?
- How do I reflect and express that treasure in my life?
- How can I pass that treasure on to my children and others within my circle?

THE GREATEST TREASURE

What is my greatest treasure? What is most precious to me?

Remember, Deuteronomy 11:1 charges the adults: "You shall therefore love the LORD your God." And verse 18 shows what that means and how it happens: "You shall therefore lay up these words of mine in your heart and in your soul." As this relationship with God is developing and this preparation has begun, then the adults are ready to teach the children about God. How do we work on this relationship and this preparation?

Once again Psalm 71 can give us some direction. How does the psalmist prepare himself to proclaim the glory of his great treasure, God?

- He leans on God, depends on him for everything, even his very life (v. 6).
- He turns to God and calls to him for help when he is in danger and needs protection (v. 7).
- He learns from God's teaching (v. 17).
- His mouth is filled with praise at the glory he sees and experiences (vv. 8, 14, 15).
- His hope, his confidence in God, is a way of life (v. 14).

REFLECTING OUR TREASURE

How do I express the greatest treasure in my life?

When we look at Psalm 71 to see what the psalmist is praising, we note some words that express what a valuable treasure God is.

- God gives us our existence and life (v. 6).
- God is our protection (v. 7).
- God's glory fills our mouths (v. 8).
- God's righteous and saving actions are immeasurable (vv. 15, 19).
- God shows us his righteousness through his mighty deeds (v. 16).
- God teaches us, our whole life long, through his wondrous deeds (v. 17).
- God's mighty power is worthy to be proclaimed to all generations (v. 18).
- God is utterly unique, unmatched—there is none like him (v. 19).

PASSING ON THE TREASURE

How can I pass that treasure on to my children and others within my circle?

Deuteronomy 11:19 tells us, "You shall teach [God's words] to your children, talking of them when you are sitting in your house, and when you are walking by the way, and when you lie down, and when you rise." Here in Psalm 71 the psalmist is an example of a person who loves to display his treasure to anyone within range. Let's see how he does it.

- He writes poems and psalms so others can read and be drawn into his praise and love and reverence for God.
- He praises God continually, all day long (vv. 6, 8).
- He acknowledges God's protection (v. 7).
- He prays for God's strength and care in the unknown future, basing his request on the kind of things God has done before (vv. 9-15).
- He hopes continually in God, which causes his praise to keep increasing (v. 14).
- He talks about what God has done and expresses his own awe (vv. 15, 19).
- He reminds others of God's righteousness, helping them remember what God has done in their lives (vv. 16, 19).
- He trusts that God will be the same through his whole life (v. 17).
- He prays for God's presence and power in his old age so that he can keep on showing God to the next generation (v. 18).

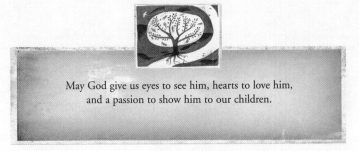

May God give us eyes to see him, hearts to love him,
and a passion to show him to our children.

A Lullaby for Talitha

Sung to the tune of "If Thou But Suffer God to Guide Thee"

Come rest your head and nestle gently,
And do not fear the dark of night;
Almighty God keeps watch intently
And guards your life with all his might.
Doubt not his love nor power to keep;
He never fails nor does he sleep.

JOHN PIPER

FIVE

"EVERYDAY" AND THE ULTIMATE

Can Daddy tuck me in? Please? Please? Please? I already brushed my teeth and went to the bathroom." Talitha throws herself onto my lap and smothers me with a hug that's meant to plead her case.

"Sure." I finally get a word in—the word she wants.

The squeeze tightens. I'm struck by a glancing kiss and released. She turns to her dad.

"Daddy! Will you take me up on your back?"

"Stand on the sofa and hold onto my neck."

They disappear up the stairs, but their voices remain audible as she's tossed onto her bed and tucked under her covers.

"Oh no!" Her laughter ends. "Where's Christopher?" In the moment of silence, I know her daddy is reaching over to find this week's favorite baby in the dolly crib and putting him in Talitha's arms.

"Daddy, will you sing me a song?" And the old familiar hymn tune settles around her, but now with new words from Daddy.

On cue, just as the last word is fading, Talitha begs, "Bless me, Daddy. Bless me."

The deeper voice is low now. I can't make out the words, but I've heard them many times before:

"*'The Lord bless you and keep you;*
the Lord make his face to shine upon you
and be gracious to you;
the Lord lift up his countenance upon you
and give you peace . . .'
and someday [From downstairs, I hear a giggle] *a godly husband!"*

Talitha's laughter erupts. The low voice speaks a quiet word. Then there's silence, after just one more outbreak. "Leave the door cracked, Daddy!"

Talitha may have the impression she's stringing Daddy along, postponing bedtime. But actually she knows exactly what to expect, what to ask for, because Daddy is following the routine he's planned for saying good night to his daughter. The script is the same every night.

We can only guess how much Talitha is soaking up at bedtime as she goes to sleep, tucked in by the love of her parents, the security of her home, and the blessing of God. We pray that the regularity and repetition and consistency of this and other routines are being used by God to shape her foundation, her assumptions, about the steadiness and dependability of God.

Learning What Their Parents Think Is Important

Our homes are the universities where our children learn about the world and how to live. What kind of basic "courses" are we offering them? As Christians, we want God to be the core of our curriculum. We want our children to be learning to know God and relate to him. God has given us his Word to help us and our children know him. And he has taught us to pray so that we can have a constant relationship with him.

Learning That God's Word Is Important

God's Word is the way God has given us to know him, our only source of life and happiness. You want to know what to do to make sure your children know the importance of God's Word? It's simple, though it seems to be one of the hardest things for families actually to do. The answer is family devotions.

Family devotions is a good example of the need to plan. It won't "just happen," at least not regularly. Someone needs to have decided when, where, what to read, who will read, and how to know what to pray for. Perhaps before Dad calls the family together, he takes five or ten minutes to look at the Bible passage and think of its main points and a couple of questions the family might ponder.

Children need basic Bible knowledge and theological understanding that develops with that knowledge. We've always thought it was important for our children to be familiar with the words and sounds of the Bible itself. So, whatever their ages, we've always had a daily time of reading directly from the Bible. That's often a time for theological conversations as they grow in their understanding. This is prime time for learning to know God's beauty, holiness, purity, sovereignty, goodness, mercy, faithfulness, wisdom, justice, wrath, and love. And it is prime time for teaching how God wants us to live.

The Bible offers everything we want most deeply for our children. Paul tells Timothy (2 Timothy 3:14-17) what he can receive from God's Word:

- wisdom
- salvation through faith in Jesus Christ
- teaching
- reproof
- correction
- training in righteousness
- competence
- equipment for every good work

> 2 TIMOTHY 3:14-17
> [14]As for you, continue in what you have learned and have firmly believed, knowing from whom you learned it [15]and how from childhood you have been acquainted with the sacred writings, which are able to make you wise for salvation through faith in Christ Jesus. [16]All Scripture is breathed out by God and profitable for teaching, for reproof, for correction, and for training in righteousness, [17]that the man of God may be competent, equipped for every good

In other words, as Paul summarizes it, children need teaching from the Bible so they can grow into men and women of God. That's what we long for on their behalf and what God offers through his Word.

A catechism can be a helpful tool. Its question-and-answer format takes a family systematically from "Who made you?" through "Does Adam's sin affect us?" to "What is heaven?" and all the basics in between. With Talitha we've used *My First Book of Questions and Answers.*[2]

For the younger children, we like to read through a Bible storybook. This helps them come to recognize the main biblical characters and their stories and to grasp basic chronology.

The evening devotional time is when our family prays together. What an encouragement it is for a child to know that his parents and siblings are praying for him! And how good it is when a child learns how to talk to God while still young. He learns to pray just as he learns most things, first by hearing others do it and then by trying it himself. For a while, learning will probably mean echoing Mom or Dad phrase by phrase in a simple prayer, but soon he'll be asking to "do it by myself."

We don't forget to eat, and we feel icky if we don't remember to brush our teeth. How wonderful it is when family worship is just as normal a part of the day—so that the day is uncomfortable and off-kilter without it.

LEARNING WHO GOD IS

A child is learning about God all week, but there is something focused and intense about being with God's people to worship in a particular place on a particular day. God knew what we needed when he inspired the words of Hebrews 10:24-25, admonishing us to meet together.

Who can measure all that a child learns by gathering regularly with God's people? There is the Word of God itself, the proclamation from the pulpit and the teaching in classes. That's the most important thing, but there's more. One small thing for our family was that we never had to teach Talitha the days of the week. She learned them by their function. First she knew Sunday, the day that anchors all the rest. Then Wednesday, when we eat supper at church and she has class with her friends. Then Saturday, the day we get ready for Sunday. Then Tuesday and Friday, the mornings Daddy's at church for early prayer when she gets up. Then Thursday, Daddy's day off. And that leaves Monday.

> HEBREWS 10:24-25
> [24]Let us consider how to stir up one another to good works, [25]not neglecting to meet together, as is the habit of some, but encouraging one another, and all the more as you see the Day drawing near.

Of course, there are more significant, though intangible, effects. We've been thankful for leadership and learning opportunities our children have had with their peers and adults in classes and youth group. During Sunday morning worship, though, they always sit with the family, even the teenagers. We worship together. Perhaps the children haven't always understood why, but my husband and I wanted our unity to say to our children and to others, "We are a family together before God. We depend on him for our lives, and we come before him together as part of the body of Christ."

This brings up the need to train young children to sit through church services. I started easing mine into the habit when they were about three. That meant sitting on the end of an out-of-the-way pew so we could slip out if we needed to. We knew that the best way for a child to learn how to worship is to see Mom and Dad worshiping. We wanted our children to be part of the whole congregation as soon as they and we could manage it. Yes, it's different for different children. And, yes, Mom's and Dad's worship is pretty distracted for a while. But that's what parents do: We live a less-than-ideal (by some standards) life for a few years so we can bring our children up to be adults with us. (For thoughts about this, see Appendix—"The Family: Together in God's Presence," p. 108.)

LEARNING HOW TO RELATE TO GOD
Relating to God Through Personal Devotions

"What do you think I am? A dog? Coming against me with sticks and stones! C'mere, kid! I'm gonna feed you to the birds!" Three-year-old Abraham, in terry cloth robe and dishtowel head covering, plastic sword in hand, growled Goliath's challenge.

Quickly he threw aside the sword and faced the other direction, becoming David, grasping his imaginary sling. "You come to me with a sword and a spear, but I come to you in the name of the Lord!"

This "reality" form of make-believe grew out of Abraham's daily morning Bible time. He couldn't read yet, and so he listened to Bible stories on tape, filling his mind and imagination with the Lord who fights for his people.

We stuck "Talitha's Morning List" to the fridge with a magnet as soon as she could *try* to read it. Each morning after Talitha has taken care of things, including "make up bed, dirty clothes down chute, breakfast, feed Sable, vitamins, brush teeth," she comes to "Bible time." At this point, she picks up her Bible and goes to a cozy corner by herself to read and pray. She knows we won't interrupt her during this quarter hour. This habit with God's Word began for her, as it did for her brothers, before she could read. Like them, she listened to Bible stories from cassettes or CDs.

It takes only a few seconds of thought to realize that it is smarter to get a three-year-old started with good lifetime habits than to spring a new regimen on a teenager. One old saying is, "As the twig is bent, so grows the tree." Wise Solomon said with the authority of Scripture: "Train up a child in the way he should go; even when he is old he will not depart from it" (Proverbs 22:6). Why would we wait to train up our children in this essential discipline? Do we think younger children don't yet need time alone with God?

That's one of the great values of God-centered traditions: A child is learning the habits he will need as an adult. When we train our children in godly patterns, godly traditions, we're helping them get ready to move with responsibility into adulthood. I can't guarantee that my children will move seamlessly from the "Bible time" I schedule for them as children into personal devotions on their own initiative as teenagers and adults. But the steadiness of a daily childhood habit is a good basis for future disciplined living.

Relating to God Through Other Prayer

"Please protect us as we travel today," we prayed before we left the motel.

Hours later a sudden, raucous clanking drove us to the road's shoulder, miles from the nearest exit. Abraham was only ten, but watching us peer under the hood, he knew what to do. "I think we should pray." And so our family stood with heads bowed, whipped by the gusts of speeding traffic, and asked God to help us.

When we opened our eyes, a pickup had stopped. The driver was a mechanic who diagnosed the problem in a moment—our water pump was shot. How would we get a new one? Everything was closed by now, and we had no transportation anyway. No problem. He drove to the twenty-four-hour truck stop where he worked, got the part, brought it back, and installed it right there beside the freeway.

On the road again, we thanked Abraham for pointing us toward God, "a very present help in trouble" (Psalm 46:1). And we thanked God for answering our roadside prayer for help.

"But what about our prayer at the motel?" Abraham's daddy asked. "Why didn't God answer *that* prayer when we asked for protection?" By the time we found that night's motel, we were still discussing how God works through our prayers. We realized we had even greater things to thank him for, because he had shown himself to us more clearly than if nothing had happened.

He *had* kept us safe—only the car was broken. He had reminded us to pray, giving us the privilege of leaning on him for help. He brought us a mechanic with ability, with access to the part we needed, and with time and willingness to help.

That also gave time for conversation with the man about our amazing God and the way he works.

Before we slept, we knew our prayers would be bigger in the morning, because God always has more to show us than we know to ask for. We knew more about God because we had talked with our children about God when we were driving along the freeway, today's version of "walking by the way" (Deuteronomy 11:19).

Relating to God Through Mealtime Prayer

Maybe the prayer habits in your family are sketchy. If so, perhaps the first step in getting regular would be to give thanks before all your meals. It's easy to flop down at the table and dig right in, to take it for granted that we always have food and to forget that it all comes from God. But remember, God doesn't like to be taken for granted.

As we Pipers gather at the table, we sit (usually not very quietly) until everyone's there. After so many meals together, no one has to tell anyone what to do next. In one movement each of us stretches both hands out to the ones on each side. We grasp hands, bow our heads, and close our eyes. Then we take our next cue from my husband. He might begin to thank God for the meal. He might ask someone else to give thanks. But most often he begins one of the family mealtime prayers we've used for years. By the third word, we're all with him, praying out loud together.

Without spelling it out, mealtime prayers remind us three times a day that God is there, filling our needs and hearing our prayers. As we give thanks, we are acknowledging that we'd have nothing without him: "Every good gift [including food] and every perfect gift is from above, coming down from the Father of lights" (James 1:17).

PIPER FAMILY
MEALTIME PRAYERS

Morning
Our Father, every day you give
The food by which our bodies live.
For this we thank you from our heart
And pray that as we this day start,
You might allow our eyes to see
Your endless generosity.
And grant that when we thus are filled,
We may do only what you've willed.

Midday
We're grateful, Father, for this hour
To rest and draw upon your power,
Which you have shown in sun and rain
And measured out to every grain.
Let all this food which you have made
And graciously before us laid
Restore our strength for these next hours
That you may have our fullest powers.

Evening
How faithful, Father, is your care;
Again as always food is there.
Again you have set us before
A meal we pray will mean much more
Than single persons filled with food;
Let there be, Lord, a loving mood.
And as you make our bodies new,
Come now and feed our oneness too.
                                    JOHN PIPER

THE IMPORTANCE OF
PARENTS' PRAYERS

Then there's another kind of prayer that our families depend on. That's the prayer we have together as a couple. We might think that isn't a family tradition that has anything to do with the kids, since it concerns what we say to God when the children aren't around. If we thought that, we'd be wrong. We're talking about superglue—the bond that makes marriages stronger, families stronger.

When my husband counsels couples in trouble, he asks them, "Do you pray together regularly?" Often they look down, shuffle their feet, and say something like, "Well, not really very regularly." I'll admit, there've been times when we two have been so angry or frustrated or discouraged with each other that when it's time to pray together, we don't know how we can do it. But you know what seems even more impossible? *Not* praying together. It's such an ingrained habit that it's blessedly inconceivable not to pray together. That's what we need—prayer that we can't *not* do together. We need a *habit* of prayer so that when praying together is hard, it's even harder to say, "Let's not."

The bonding that happens in *our* prayers is a gift from God to our children. And there are other gifts to them in our prayers. If we both pray for each other every day, our prayers are one of God's ways of granting our children better parents. And we must never forget, each of our children needs us to pray for him or her every day. Then as the Lord adds daughters-in-law, sons-in-law, and grandchildren to our families, our prayers expand.

Here's another gift our children may receive through the regularity of our just-the-two-of-us prayer. We don't pray "that [we] may be seen by others," as Jesus put it (Matthew 6:5). But there are times that a child does see us kneeling beside our bed

---

O LORD, MAKE ABER GREAT!

How many times I've stood beside
Your bed when you're asleep, and tried
To find the words for my desire:
That you might be a living fire
For God. Sometimes I say, "O Lord,
Make Aber great! Open your Word
And let him see enough to break
His heart and then, for Jesus' sake,
To heal with remedies of grace;
And give him strength to run his race."

And when I see you up before
The sun, to read God's Word and store
Up truth inside your heart and mind,
I thank the Lord that he is kind.

Sometimes when you're asleep, I touch
Your face. If you could know how much
The warmth of your life means to me!
For every freckle . . . let me see . . .
Perhaps a million dollars? . . . No.
They're not for sale! And for the glow
In your calm face there is no price.
Which means I have a very nice
And costly treasure lying here.
It's what we mean when we say, "Dear."

Tonight I'll probably just stare
At you and marvel that you're there
Asleep, and that you've just turned eight,
And say, "O Lord, make Aber great!"
    BY DADDY (JOHN PIPER), 12-12-87

together—maybe a teenager coming home late in the evening or a younger one up for the bathroom. We don't say, "Look at us. We're praying." But our children know, and we pray it will be an example they carry into their own marriages.

PRAYER IS NOT OPTIONAL

Huge things are at stake in our prayers. The salvation of our children is in God's hands. It is good that we exert ourselves to help them see and understand God. But nothing we do has any ultimate impact, except for God's Spirit working on their behalf. It is the Holy Spirit who makes the soil of their hearts fertile and ready for the seeds we plant. One plants, another waters, but only God gives the growth (1 Corinthians 3:7). So for our children we "pray that the eyes of [their] heart may be enlightened, so that [they] may know what is the hope of His calling, what are the riches of the glory of His inheritance in the saints" (Ephesians 1:18 NASB).

Many everyday activities in our lives—even excellent, God-centered activities—are optional. But some are too close to the heart of God to be left to choice. Deuteronomy 11 has shown us that God's command to us is that we love the Lord our God and serve him with all our heart and with all our soul (v. 13). In order for that to happen, he has told us, "You shall therefore lay up these words of mine in your heart and in your soul" (v. 18).

The practical necessity for this "laying up" is even more obvious when we realize the kind of interaction God expects adults to have with children: "You shall teach [God's words] to your children, talking of them when you are sitting in your house, and when you are walking by the way, and when you lie down, and when you rise" (v. 19). Our mouths are able to be filled with God's words only as much as our hearts are.

God is the most precious heirloom our children can ever receive, and receiving him means knowing and loving him. Our personal habits and family traditions of the Word and prayer are the ones that are not optional if we want God as our eternal inheritance.

Our mouths will be filled with God's words
only as much as our hearts are.

SIX

"EVERYDAY" TRADITIONS, THE FAMILY, AND THE WORLD

God's Word and prayer are at the heart of some of our "everyday" traditions, as we saw in the previous chapter. What are some of the other, though less "ultimate," lessons to be learned through the regular patterns in a family? Maybe if we think about some of the things our children are learning through their daily lives, it will give us ideas and impetus to develop new family habits or strengthen old ones. This chapter will not be an exhaustive list of "what a Christian family ought to be doing." Instead, please read these examples as illustrations to help you think about your family through God's eyes and to help open your eyes more clearly to God through your life together.

LEARNING WHO AND WHAT THEIR FAMILY IS

"Tell us a Quintle and Quinjy story, Daddy!" Young Karsten or Benjamin made this request every time they rode with Daddy in the car. So Daddy would create a story of adventure and danger, his brain running only a couple of words ahead of his mouth. Quintle, who was just the age of Karsten, and Quinjy, the same age as Benjamin, always found themselves in a scrape, in catastrophes involving waterfalls, earthquakes, airplanes, and toppling buildings. They would be saved through either Quintle's logical deliberation or Quinjy's impulsive agility, or—in the best stories— by both of them together. As the boys grew, the fictional predicaments became more impossible, and a new character appeared on the scene. The boys needed only to cry desperately, "Balo-o-o-^{ney}!" and Baloney, the phenomenal pony, no matter how far away he was, arrived in a galloping rush to manage their rescue.

There are other evidences, besides stories, that we Pipers are a word-oriented family. When we sit around the table, comments and arguments shoot from one person to another. On his day off, my husband and I play Scrabble. Karsten teaches English. Benjamin is a poised and natural speaker. When Abraham sleeps late, he loses his chance at the daily newspaper crossword because I beat him to it. Books are near the top of Barnabas's Christmas list. One Christmas recently, he asked for *The Works of Jonathan Edwards* and his own set of the Narnia books. If we can't find Talitha, she's probably curled up somewhere reading. I love it when it's some favorite from my own childhood, like *The Five Little Peppers* or *The Secret Garden* or *Heidi*.

I expect our children will remember childhood word games in the car. "What's the opposite of upside down?" "Does anything rhyme with orange?" "How can flammable and inflammable mean the same thing?"

And books. I wish I knew how many I've read to our children. I wonder if they'll always associate the sound of a good book with the smell of fresh laundry. When their drawers had become empty, and all their clothes were washed and in the clean clothes mountain, we'd sort everything into separate piles, one for each child. Then while they folded, I read.

My up-front motive was a fair trade: "You're doing what I want, and I'm doing what you want." But what else was happening? They were learning to sort, learning to be responsible for their own clothes, learning to work and listen at the same time. Those are helpful skills, but we all know the most valuable lessons are deeper and less tangible.

When we read to our children, at the deeper level they are learning about life. They're soaking up what we think about world events, what it takes to be a real hero, how important it is to act with integrity. Sometimes we have to stop and talk about what we read. Maybe a character we like acts in a way that puzzles us. How could Laura and her family think a black-faced minstrel show was so much fun? Or maybe a character we don't like doesn't seem to get what he deserves. How does Templeton get by with being such a . . . rat? From those stories and conversations, our children are gaining a sense of who their family is, and thus who they are.

Do your children ever ask you to tell them about when you were little? When they listen to your stories, they're learning history, beginning at a very personal level. And they're finding out what shapes a person into an adult who follows Christ. Like when I was a kid, and the school burned down one weekend. Lost in the blaze were the birthstone necklace I wasn't supposed to have worn to school and the spelling book I was supposed to have taken home for homework. My children remember all too well the account of my disobedience and downfall.

The stories we tell and the books we choose are influenced by the gender, ages, and interests of our children, from Andersen and Seuss to Lewis and Lawhead. An additional ingredient was stirred in when our family became interracial through our adoption of Talitha. Since then we've discovered history and heroes we should have known before. (Did you know that Betsey Stockton, America's first single woman missionary, was a freed slave?[3])

That's *our* family. The enjoyment of words that God gave us helps us realize how important words are. God used a book full of words to tell us about himself. God the Son is even called "the Word." If we didn't have words, how could we understand God and his world? What a precious gift to be a "word family"!

Who is your family? What habits and traditions do you enjoy together that express your family's character and help you see that facet of God? Maybe you're artistic, and you feel a special connection with the colors and designs God uses to paint and shape our world. Maybe you're a family who builds, and you relate to God especially as creator. Maybe you travel, fix things, or work the farm or the garden.

Think about it, not to become self-conscious, but rather to consider how God is reflected in your family and in the activities you especially enjoy.

LEARNING ORDER IN LIFE

With a mouth full of ramen noodles, Talitha asks, "What are we going to read today?" Most days after lunch, we sit together and I read to her, maybe from a library book and maybe from the next chapter of *Sir Gibbie*. She doesn't have to ask, "Are we going to read?" She knows what to expect.

When our children were preschoolers, they knew the order of the morning because it was the same almost every day. After some playing came lunch and then naptime. The clock was nothing; sequence was everything. This meant that if I wanted them happy when I had to take them somewhere in the early afternoon, I could feed them at 10:30 or 11:00, and they'd nap before our outing.

Our regular "everyday" traditions give shape and order to our days. Even the most spontaneous person needs some predictability in his life. God is not the author of chaos. Our children are soaking in some of his character when there are at least a few regular patterns and traditions in our homes.

LEARNING TO RELATE TO THE WORLD OUTSIDE THE HOME
Decision-making

"But, Daddy, what's wrong with . . . ?" Familiar question. And a parent's easy retort might be, "What's right with it?" That's catchy and has some truth, but maybe we can help our children dig a little deeper into the mind of God when they need to make decisions.

Some traditions are not events and are not on a regular schedule. Sometimes a tradition is words that you know you will hear in a certain situation. If our children ask my husband, "What's wrong with . . . ?" they know what he'll answer. He'll say, "That's the wrong question. Here's what you need to be asking: Will it strengthen my faith and help me love Jesus more?" Those are the basic filters. Depending on the circumstances, there may be other ways of asking the same filter-questions: Will it advance me in my warfare against sin? Will it help me be more resolved to pray? Will it embolden my witness?

Our children's lives will be filled with decisions as they mature. The way we help them assess their earlier, less crucial choices is training for what is to come. And think about those questions—we parents haven't outgrown them either. Let's try to ingrain those filter-questions into our children while they're young so that choosing godly options is a lot easier and more natural for them than maybe it's been for us.

Hospitality

For some people a meal set for six or seven is a full table that involves lots of planning and preparation. I think of a cozy dining room like that when I remember some Sundays at our house. If our boys came home from church and saw the table ready for six or seven—our family—at least one was sure to exclaim in disbelief, "Nobody's here? Why isn't anybody here?" That's how accustomed they were to Sunday guests at our table and how much they enjoyed it. They viewed home as a place where visitors come and go, where their friends are welcome, where others get swept into our family's hubbub of conversation over a plate of spaghetti or bowl of soup.

Hospitality's conversations aren't all with invited guests either. Some talks occur at the door with pairs of sect members wanting to proselytize. Some conversations are on the phone with a troubled person who needs prayer. Some are on the front porch with a street person who thinks he needs just food and drink.

We may try to teach our children that the "earth is the LORD's and the fullness thereof, the world and those who dwell therein" (Psalm 24:1). They may memorize the words and meditate on them. But they learn what the words mean when they see in their own home that our family and our home and our food and our stuff and our time are not ours. They are the Lord's, and that means these things are available for his purposes of love.

Learning How God and Parents See the World

"When I grow up, I'm going to be the kind of missionary who is a juggler and pianist and soccer player and actor . . . in China." Benjamin's dreams were as wildly diverse as any ten-year-old's. And as a young world Christian, he already assumed that his future could be anywhere in the world. What were some of the things that had opened his eyes to see beyond the downtown Minneapolis neighborhood where we'd lived as long as he could remember?[4]

The first thing was one of those you-always-say-that responses—the answer Benjamin knew he'd hear when he asked school geography questions or when a place was discussed on a radio program or when we received mail from friends far away in California or Cameroon: "Let's find it on the map." And the map was on the wall, readily accessible. (Our world map eventually "grew" into a wallpaper mural covering one whole wall of our dining room.)

Another "everyday" tradition was part of our family prayer. Benjamin regularly heard us praying for missionaries and for unreached peoples who need the gospel. These prayers worked at least two ways in his mind and heart. The first was a reminder of the *world* part of *world Christian*—that our city and neighborhood

NOW WE'RE COOKIN'

Noël's Spaghetti

This is a family favorite, the choice for most
birthday dinners, and a perfect make-ahead. I make a
huge batch—for about fifteen adults. The recipe can
easily be cut into thirds.

3 lb. ground meat	1 tsp. black pepper
1 Tbs. whole oregano	1 Tbs. basil
1 Tbs. garlic powder	2-3 bay leaves
1 Tbs. salt	
3 Tbs. dried parsley	

2 Tbs. Worcestershire sauce

1 large onion (or 1/3 cup dry onion flakes)

Institutional size can tomato sauce (six 15-oz. cans)

6-10 drops Tabasco sauce (optional)

Brown meat. Drain. Stir in flavorings and
spices. Add tomato sauce. Simmer at least one-half
hour.

Noël's secret to non-sticky pasta: (Use about
twice as much as the pasta package says. Cook until
done but not overdone. Strain. Immediately rinse
with cold water until noodles are cold. With hands,
mix in oil to coat pasta (about 2 Tbs. per pound).
Cover well until ready to use, up to a day ahead.
Heat in microwave.

are only one part of God's large world that's filled with many kinds of people. The other was a piece of the *Christian* part of *world Christian*—the truth of Jesus' reminder that "I am the way, and the truth, and the life. No one comes to the Father except through me" (John 14:6). A helpful daily tool for this kind of prayer is *The Global Prayer Digest.*[5] In fact, world missions leader Ralph Winter once said that the reason he helped conceive and promote the *Digest* was that the things that have the longest and deepest effect on people's lives are the things they do every day. Praying daily for a different unreached-people group gets missions under the skin.

LEARNING THEIR PLACE IN THE FAMILY
Names

"What shall we name him? Jonathan Daniel. Daniel William. William Jonathan. Barnabas Daniel. Barnabas William. Yes! He's Barnabas William."

I squeezed the hand of my husband and raised my head from the pillow to kiss the damp, dark hair of the wrinkly, red, almost ten-pound ball of baby nestled on my chest.

"That was fast," the nurse commented.

Not really. We'd discussed these possibilities for months, and each was special to us because of the person and qualities it represented. Our difficulty was not finding a name, but narrowing the list to only two.

A child hears his name dozens of times a day, hundreds of times a week, thousands of times a year. In some way, it defines who he is. So it has been the habit—the tradition—of my husband and me to choose our children's names carefully. Karsten Luke's name reflects the stage of our lives when he was born. We were in Germany; so his name is a German variation of *Christian*. Benjamin John's name is a prayer that he will indeed be a "son of his father's right hand." Abraham Christian has big sandals to fill, to follow God with the faith of Abraham. In Barnabas

Announcing the birth

Our second son is BENJAMIN JOHN.

Beloved by God, he dwells secure
Upon a cosmic boulder;
Though small and to the world obscure,
He rides on Yahweh's shoulder.
Deuteronomy 33:12

September 1, 1975; 9 lb., 1 oz.; 21.5 in.

John & Noël Piper

P.S. Unlike Rachel, Noël is doing fine.

William, we honor his Opa, William Piper, a man whose life has been shaped by his calling to spread the gospel.

Talitha Ruth's name is a story of adoption. Talitha, "which means 'Little girl'" (Mark 5:41)—this family has been given a little girl. Ruth, Talitha's adoptive grandmother—this little girl has been given a family.

Each of us bears the name *Piper*, which means "you're part of this particular family; you're ours and we're yours." We pray that all our children will also come to bear the name *Christian*, meaning "you're part of the family of Christ; you're his and he's yours."

As we talk with our children about the meaning of their names, we're giving them examples and standards to aspire to, as many parents did in the Bible. We help a child know the importance of his own name when we tell about the Shepherd who knows each name: "The sheep hear his voice, and he calls his own sheep by name" (John 10:3). And he never forgets us; when we are his, our names are recorded forever in the Book of Life (Revelation 3:5).

Special Music

"Daddy! Do you have your hymnal?" Talitha squirms and stretches her arm across him to reach his PDA as he pulls it from his pocket. She flips open the cover, clicks out the stylus, and runs the device through its paces until she reaches the menu of songs Daddy has saved. She scrolls down until she reaches the one she wants tonight, and we sing together. This routine is part of our evening devotions, between the Bible storybook and prayers.

Although we would have said for many years that most of us in this household are not very musical, music is an important part of our "everyday" traditions. Right after our evening prayers is bedtime, and another song is part of the tucking-in routine (p. 42).

Each of our children has his or her own special hymn, the one I sang most regularly as a lullaby when the child was a baby. I had just memorized "Great Is Thy Faithfulness"; so that came most easily to my lips when I was desperate to quiet baby Karsten. Psalm 23 was fresh in my mind when Benjamin was born; so for him I learned "The Lord's My Shepherd." For Abraham how could I resist "The God of Abraham Praise"? Soon after Barnabas was born, an ensemble at church sang "O Let Your Soul Now Be Filled with Gladness," the first time I'd ever heard it. The lilting tune and confident message so perfectly enveloped and lifted the sad moment of the second verse; it made me cry and helped to lighten my short-lived "baby blues." When we adopted Talitha, I searched for a hymn that assures her of a permanent, faithful home and found it in "Children of the Heavenly Father."

I often sang their songs to my little ones at bedtime. Nowadays in church, I have to look up to the older ones to share the glance that says, "They're singing your song"—your song of our faithful, glad Shepherd-Father God.

By the way, our formerly mostly non-musical family now includes two guitarists, a budding pianist, some vocalists on stage or in worship teams or choirs . . . and some who still sound best in extremely large groups.

A Child's Own History

"Abraham! Look what I just found in your file. Remember that bike-a-thon for school when you didn't ride as far as you said you were going to? Here's the letter Grand-daddy wrote you saying he didn't want his extra money back."

Abraham at twenty-something doesn't remember. But because of the "Abraham" file my organized husband keeps, there are words here for all of us in my father's own handwriting:

O Let Your Soul Now Be Filled with Gladness

O let your soul now be filled with gladness,
Your heart redeemed, rejoice indeed!
O may the thought banish all your sadness
That in his blood you have been freed,
That God's unfailing love is yours,
That you the only Son were given,
That by his death he has opened heaven,
That you are ransomed as you are.

If you seem empty of any feeling,
Rejoice—you are his ransomed bride!
If those you cherish seem not to love you,
And dark assails from every side,
Still yours the promise, come what may,
In loss and triumph, in laughter, crying,
In want and riches, in living, dying,
That you are purchased as you are.

It is a good every good transcending
That Christ has died for you and me!
It is a gladness that has no ending
Therein God's wondrous love to see!
Praise be to him, the spotless Lamb,
Who through the desert my soul is leading
To that fair city of joy exceeding,
For which he bought me as I am.

PETER JONSSON ASCHAN

I encourage you to always set your goals higher than you think you can reach and then work diligently to reach the goal. You will miss it many times, but you will also reach it many times. In the Lord's work, goals are reached by prayer and much work. Our children and grandchildren give us much joy, and we love you all very much.

By now there are several folders for each of our children, filled with certificates, drawings, letters, photographs, poems, creative writing, report cards, newspaper clippings, and whatever we want to keep. To open one of these manila files is better than peeking into a treasure chest.

There's the letter young Benjamin wrote to his grandmother, for example (and that she gave back to us later): "Dear Gma, Thak you for 5 dolars. I like mony and I love you." When we read that, someone is sure to say, "Remember how Mother always made us write at least two sentences in our thank-you notes?"

A lot of love and history lives in those file folders—history that one particular child can "read" to know more about who he is in this particular God-loving family.

LEARNING HOW TO BE ADULTS

"Nobody is stronger than you, Daddy," Talitha states with confidence. Her daddy knows better; so he's teaching her to depend on her heavenly Father. It's absolutely true that there's nobody stronger than *he* is. But even though the best possible daddy can't compare with our heavenly Father, still God uses fathers to teach children what he himself is like.

> 2 CORINTHIANS 6:18
> "And I will be a father to you, and you shall be sons and daughters to me," says the Lord Almighty.
>
> HEBREWS 12:9-10
> 9Besides this, we have had earthly fathers who disciplined us and we respected them. Shall we not much more be subject to the Father of spirits and live? 10For they disciplined us for a short time as it seemed best to them, but he disciplines us for our good, that we may share his holiness.

The Bible is filled with references to God as Father. He promises to be a father to his people, as in 2 Corinthians 6:18. Hebrews 12:9-10 shows how the example of our earthly fathers helps us know the way to relate to God.

What sort of everyday traditions help children understand God more clearly so that they can grow up to be adults who depend on God? For years the evening mealtime conversation at our house has included debate about what to do during "playtime." Our children know that right after supper Daddy does whatever (almost) the children want, from reading to being a bucking bronco. We gave up on having a nice backyard lawn because it was incompatible with frequent kickball and soccer games. And anyway what's more important? When Daddy's down on the floor playing with Talitha's dollhouse, she's seeing a reflection of the Incarnation—God stooping to our level so that we can relate to him and understand him.

Another example is Saturday lunch dates with Daddy. Each child knows what to expect over the pizza when his or her turn comes. There'll be fun conversation about the child's current interests. Daddy will ask how things are going. He'll probe a bit into something in that son's or daughter's life that he is concerned about. He'll have some loving, good advice. Someday I hope our children will realize that when it was their turn with Daddy, he was showing them a father who likes to be with his children, one on one, who cares about what's important to his child, and whose words are wise and helpful—like God.

These times with the children are a reminder of the importance of planning. It might seem coldhearted to write "playtime with children" on your calendar, but really it's a loving way to make sure that a good thing happens, a time that you and your children enjoy. Scheduling helps you respond to competing requests. You can look at your calendar and say, "Sorry, I have another appointment at that time." Both you and the children may take it for granted after a while, but the tradition wouldn't have developed if you hadn't planned it into your days. When your children know they can depend on Dad and Mom, it will be much easier for them to learn to depend on God.

Being this kind of parent may not come easy for a person whose own father or mother was far from God, disinterested, or abusive. But in their own way, indirectly, poor parents also point us toward God and how to be the kind of parents we ought to be. At the least, their example shows us the kind of parent we *don't* want to be. But more directly, their failures leave us realizing that God is the one we lean on. "For my father and my mother have forsaken me, but the LORD will take me in" (Psalm 27:10). As parents, we can be in no better position than leaning on God and showing our children the dependability and love of a heavenly Father who never lets us down.

When your children know they can depend on Dad and Mom,
it will be much easier for them to learn to depend on God.

Celebrations are the ritualized interruptions
in the continuum of daily life
which remind us who we are,
where we came from and where we are going.

MILO SHANNON-THORNBERRY,
The Alternate Celebrations Catalogue[6]

SEVEN

"ESPECIALLY" TRADITIONS

WE NEED "ESPECIALLY"

No!" our college friend squawked. "All days are *not* the same! God knows we need 'especially.'"

He'd heard it once too often, somebody pontificating, "Every day should be Mother's Day," or "Every day should be as significant as Christmas."

God knows we need "especially"—that was a new thought to me back then. And it's true. God himself appointed special days, such as Passover, for his people and gave them ceremonies to set those days off from the others (Exodus 12:1-20). December 25, for example, could pass like any other day in our week, except for the thought and preparation we give to it and the customs and traditions that surround it. The ceremony of a special day keeps it from slipping away like an ordinary day. We stop and recognize the specialness of an event in large part because of the traditions in which it's wrapped.

Our "especially" celebrations anchor us and our children in the harbor of our family, reflecting our true refuge—God. The way we observe these occasions—the focus of our observation—has great potential to show our children what we think is most important and to help them value what we hold most dear. Of course, the benefits are not just for the children. Our celebrations work good in our own lives and in other people whose lives touch ours, by rekindling our love of God, by increasing our knowledge of him, and by helping us remember who God is and how he works.

LOOKING BACKWARD AND FORWARD

Memory is the mother of traditions. Almost all of our special days are celebrated because they remind us of something significant in the past. A birthday looks back to a birth. An anniversary looks back to a wedding. A funeral looks back on a life. Christmas looks back on Jesus' birth. Easter looks back to his death and resurrection. Our celebrations are occasions to look back and remember what God has done in the world and in our lives.

At the same time, we are also looking forward. The preparations we make and the eagerness we feel as we look ahead toward a special day are a foretaste of the emotions we will experience when we encounter God in a special way as we celebrate. And that encounter with God is, in turn, a foreshadowing of the great day when we will see him face to face.

Memory and anticipation swirl together before a great occasion. When Barnabas was younger, he wondered before his birthday, "Will the poem Daddy writes for me this year be funny or spiritual?" Perhaps he hadn't caught on yet that even Daddy's funny poems are also spiritual. But what he had caught onto was this:

Every year Daddy wrote a poem for his birthday. As Barnabas looked forward to the celebration of his day, he knew what to expect because of his memory of "the way it always is." His memory of earlier birthdays increased his anticipation of the celebration yet to come.

At the Heart of Every Celebration

Thinking of birthdays raises an important question. Some of our most significant events—birthdays, weddings, anniversaries, funerals—honor particular people. At those times, how do we demonstrate that *God* is at the heart of every celebration? Can we honor God appropriately while focusing so much attention on people? How do we keep God at the center? We can answer those questions in various ways. Paul said, "In him we live and move and have our being" (Acts 17:18); "For from him and through him and to him are all things. To him be glory forever. Amen" (Romans 11:36).

Through him we have birth and life and every thing and every person in our lives. So God is the reason we have *anything* to celebrate. He is the ultimate source of any of our celebrations. As we read in James 1:17, "Every good gift and every perfect gift is from above, coming down from the Father of lights with whom there is no variation or shadow due to change."

When we realize that the child, the spouse, the life, the friends, and the family are all gifts from our Father, it makes every celebration a "thanksgiving" day, a time to express our heart of thanks to God.

Saint Augustine said something that might help us when we worry that making much of a person might somehow be competition for our love of God.

BARNABAS AT SIX
I know a brand-new six-year-old.
When he was made, they tossed the mold.
That means he's just one of a kind.
Look high and low; you'll never find
In all the world another lad
Who makes a more contented dad.
Who might this rare young fellow be?
I'll give you clues so you can see:

He talks a lot. He even talks
When no one's there to hear. He walks
With courage through the battlefields
Of bedrooms, halls, and stairs, and wields
His ever-present plastic sword
To slay the beast and evil lord
That lurks behind the rocking chair
And falls dead like a grizzly bear.

Sometimes his brothers think he's cute,
With brown bowtie and little suit.
And then he tries hard not to smile;
He tries but misses by a mile.

Sometimes you'll find him with his back
Against a pillow, with a stack
Of Bible books, and on the tape
A story of some great escape
God gave to Joseph or to Paul;
And this young lad has learned them all.

I think, perhaps, that's all you need
To guess his name, but one more lead:
He has a kind of pleasant roar;
We sometimes call him Number Four.
We're glad that he is one of us:
His name? You're right. It's Barnabas.

JOHN PIPER, MARCH 31, 1989

For he loves Thee too little who loves anything together with Thee, which he loves not for Thy sake.[7]

In other words, as my husband explains, "If created things are seen and handled as gifts of God and as mirrors of his glory, they need not be occasions of idolatry— if our delight in them is always also a delight in their Maker."[8] Thinking about a few special days might help us see how this truth can play out.

BIRTHDAY

The psalmist pictures God in Psalm 139 as an author. In his mind God creates a person and the details of every day of that person's life. Then God writes the story in his book. "Your eyes saw my unformed substance; in your book were written, every one of them, the days that were formed for me, when as yet there were none of them" (v. 16). The amazing thing about this Author and his book is that once you've been thought of by God, it is certain that you will *be*. He creates not just an idea, but a flesh-and-blood person knitted together within the flesh-and-blood body of a mother.

> PSALM 139:13-18
> 13For you formed my inward parts;
> you knitted me together in my mother's womb.
> 14I praise you, for I am fearfully and wonderfully made.
> Wonderful are your works; my soul knows it very well.
> 15My frame was not hidden from you,
> when I was being made in secret,
> intricately woven in the depths of the earth.
> 16Your eyes saw my unformed substance;
> in your book were written, every one of them,
> the days that were formed for me,
> when as yet there were none of them.
> 17How precious to me are your thoughts, O God!
> How vast is the sum of them!
> 18If I would count them, they are more than the sand.
> I awake, and I am still with you.

God knows each atom of your body because he designed and created each one and wove it together with all the others. When the weaving was completed, then came the one day, from among all the days that were formed for this creature, that God appointed as the day of birth.

How would a birthday celebration change if we looked at our birthday person and imagined God's hands knitting him or her together, if we thought of his or her unabridged story written in God's book, if we remembered that this day was chosen by God specifically for this person? At the least, we would speak our personal thanks to God and lift our praising hearts to him. Then we might try to plan a time to pray with and for the birthday person, especially thanking God for him or her and asking God's blessing, recognizing that each of the person's days is written in God's book.

This is the one day of the year that belongs especially to the birthday person. We want to shower our love on a child on his or her day. Every bit of love we give

Chocolate Éclair Cake

1-lb. box graham crackers

3 small boxes instant vanilla pudding

4 c. milk

8 oz. whipped topping, thawed

Mix pudding with milk. Fold in whipped topping. Make a single layer of graham crackers to cover the bottom of a 9 x 13 pan. Cover with half of the pudding mixture. Repeat layers. Cover with final layer of grahams. Frost.

Frosting

1/2 c. unsweetened cocoa powder

2 tsp. white corn syrup

2 tsp. vanilla

1 c. powdered sugar

3 Tbs. softened margarine

3 Tbs. milk

Beat until smooth. Frosting will spread better if cake has been refrigerated a couple of hours, but cooling first is not absolutely necessary. Refrigerate cake, covered, twenty-four hours before serving. Makes 12-15 servings.

comes from God. Ours is only a pale reflection of God's love, but it is one of the means God uses to point our child toward himself.

At the Piper house, the birthday child wakes up to balloons and breakfast cake (p. 14) with candles to blow out. He or she gets to choose the menu for birthday dinner. Once we mature past the wieners and beans or macaroni and cheese stage, it's usually spaghetti (p. 56) and chocolate éclair cake. In between the cake and presents, Daddy reads the poem he's written for the occasion. Close to the birthday we try to have a family outing that the birthday child chooses—maybe miniature golf or the zoo or the science museum. Along the way, there are bound to be stories of "the day you were born." These are ways we try to say, "We are thankful for you. We love you. We are thrilled God gave you to us."

GOTCHA DAY

In many families the recounting of God's gift isn't entitled "The Day You Were Born." It might go more like this:

"Talitha, want to hear a story?" She scrambles into my lap. Fingering her beaded braids, I begin.

"A long time ago there was a little boy named Johnny and a little girl named Noël." Talitha's dark eyes light up, and she nestles into place, knowing what comes next.

"When they grew up, they fell in love and got married. After a while God gave them a fat, blond baby boy named Karsten. Then he gave them a fat, blond baby boy named Benjamin. Then he gave them a fat, blond baby boy named Abraham. Then he gave them the fattest, blondest baby, named Barnabas. Their daddy called them the cookie-cutter kids.

> GALATIANS 4:4-7
> [4]When the fullness of time had come, God sent forth his Son, born of woman, born under the law, [5]to redeem those who were under the law, so that we might receive adoption as sons. [6]And because you are sons, God has sent the Spirit of his Son into our hearts, crying, "Abba! Father!" [7]So you are no longer a slave, but a son, and if a son, then an heir through God.

"Noël and Johnny loved their boys very much. They said, 'Father in heaven, thank you so much for our sons. You have given us more than we could have dreamed. We are very happy.' Then they whispered, because they didn't want to be greedy, 'Do you think there might be a little girl for us, too?'"

I continue the familiar story of our long-distance telephone introduction to a tiny baby girl, our decision to adopt her, the preparations we made, and the day we waited and waited and *waited* until Miss Phoebe arrived and laid that little girl in our arms. "Here's your little girl."

"We squeezed her and said, 'Welcome, Talitha Ruth.' She smiled at us and . . .

burped!" Talitha chimes in on the "chorus": "Barnabas la-a-ughed and laughed. And Abraham said, 'Coo-ul!'"

Some adoptive families celebrate Gotcha Day on the anniversaries of the day they received their child. After cake and other goodies, they pull out photos and the video of "the day we gotcha." This special day is a reminder of the thanks they feel toward God for the gift of their child. He is the one who gives them the privilege of picturing the relationship he has with his children: "God sent forth his Son . . . so that we might receive adoption" (Galatians 4:4-5).

WEDDING

We shouldn't be surprised to discover that *the* original human kinship—that of Adam with Eve—is also a picture. Marriage was designed by God to be an illustration of the most important relationship we can ever have. The apostle Paul explains, "I am saying that it refers to Christ and the church" (Galatians 5:32). That statement gives marriage a significance far beyond any other human alliance we might ever make. We all realize that marriage is not God's best plan for everyone. But for those whom God leads into this bond, there is the responsibility and privilege of living a parable.

And so a wedding, though it lasts only a few moments, is eternally momentous because of the way the marriage will reflect truth or untruth about our eternal God. People who observe a marriage will have a clearer or foggier understanding of who Christ is, in part because of what they see; and that understanding has eternal implications for their lives. Could it be that one of the reasons there is so little respect for Christ and his church is that there is so little to respect in many marriages? It is certainly true that marriage is held in such light regard because its parable-purpose is almost forgotten.

Etiquette provides rules for how a wedding "should" be done. A desire for a God-centered ceremony goes beyond these rules

> EPHESIANS 5:22-33
> 22Wives, submit to your own husbands, as to the Lord. 23For the husband is the head of the wife even as Christ is the head of the church, his body, and is himself its Savior. 24Now as the church submits to Christ, so also wives should submit in everything to their husbands.
> 25Husbands, love your wives, as Christ loved the church and gave himself up for her, 26that he might sanctify her, having cleansed her by the washing of water with the word, 27so that he might present the church to himself in splendor, without spot or wrinkle or any such thing, that she might be holy and without blemish. 28In the same way husbands should love their wives as their own bodies. He who loves his wife loves himself. 29For no one ever hated his own flesh, but nourishes and cherishes it, just as Christ does the church, 30because we are members of his body. 31"Therefore a man shall leave his father and mother and hold fast to his wife, and the two shall become one flesh." 32This mystery is profound, and I am saying that it refers to Christ and the church. 33However, let each one of you love his wife as himself, and let the wife see that she respects her husband.

and asks questions to help a couple make choices that reflect the focal point of their lives and the life they will share after the ceremony.

- What is our greatest treasure? What is most precious to us?
- How do we reflect and express that treasure in our lives and in our life together?
- How can we pass that treasure on to others within our circle?

Perhaps the new bride and groom learned to ask such questions from their parents through years of family celebrations.

In what other ways are we parents helping our children prepare for marriage? Here our "everyday" traditions overlap with our "especially" occasions. One important way we help our children get ready for marriage is by teaching God's words to them every day, speaking these words when our children are sitting in our house, when they are walking by the way, when they lie down, and when they rise (Deuteronomy 11:19). Even when children are young, we can be discussing what words like these mean:

"If anyone comes to me and does not hate his own father and mother and wife and children and brothers and sisters, yes, and even his own life, he cannot be my disciple."

(LUKE 14:26)

LOVE HER MORE
AND LOVE HER LESS
(Excerpt)
For Karsten Luke
at his wedding to
Rochelle Ann Orvis
May 29, 1995

The God whom we have loved, and in
Whom we have lived, and who has been
Our Rock these twenty-two good years
With you, now bids us, with sweet tears,
To let you go: "A man shall leave
His father and his mother, cleave
Henceforth unto his wife, and be
One unashaméd flesh and free."
This is the word of God today,
And we are happy to obey.
For God has given you a bride
Who answers every prayer we've cried
For over twenty years, our claim
For you, before we knew her name.
BY DAD (JOHN PIPER)

Do not be unequally yoked with unbelievers.

(2 CORINTHIANS 6:14)

You shall not commit adultery.

(EXODUS 20:14)

Then the man said, "This at last is bone of my bones and flesh of my flesh; she shall be called Woman, because she was taken out of Man." Therefore a man shall leave his father and his mother and hold fast to his wife, and they shall become one flesh.

(GENESIS 2:23-24)

As with most of life, our sponge-like young children are soaking up their basic understanding of marriage by living in our home. When Paul tells us that our marriages are pictures of the relationship of Christ and the church, let's remember that our own children absorb almost full strength the truth or untruth reflected in our union. That is an awesome responsibility, reminding us of our "everyday" need for prayer, asking God to keep us pure and strong and true together.

Let me mention one other prayer that is a preparation for our children's future. From the time we realized we were expecting each of our children, whether by birth or adoption, we began to intercede for the little girl or boy who would grow up to be our daughter- or son-in-law, if God plans marriage for our child. We ask especially that God will bring that future spouse to a strong faith in Christ and keep him or her pure, and that God bring the two together when his time is right for them.

FUNERAL

My cousin Henry looked at the broom in my hand, glanced over at my sister setting out lunch for his family, and then above the roar of the lawn mower my brother was pushing outside, said, "This is way above and beyond . . ."

I looked him in the eye and said, "No, it isn't. We're family, and this is what family does. I learned how to do this from your parents, you know." I told him about the aunts and uncles surrounding us when Daddy died. Now Uncle Sam was gone, and we were there to surround Henry and the rest of Uncle Sam's family. It seemed like the natural thing to do.

Soon cousins from farther away arrived with ice and food and willing hands. I took a break to sit with Ruth, Henry's sister, who unwittingly disenchanted me because she knew you can't take family support for granted. "I just wish my husband could have experienced something like this when his father died," she mused. "He was about the only one there."

It may seem strange to include a funeral on the list of "especially" occasions. But the days around a funeral may be a time when we see most clearly how God has shaped a family through its traditions. Then we may be able to see more clearly how the character of God is reflected in the life of a family.

We who are grieving, how do we respond to the people who were closest to the one who died?

For as in one body we have many members, and the members do not all have the same function, so we, though many, are one body in Christ, and individually members one of another. Having gifts that differ according to the grace given to us, let us use them.

(ROMANS 12:4-6)

We will have different ways of responding. But if we are part of the body of Christ, he will be serving and comforting through our hands and words.

And if it is we who are the closest to the one who is gone, how do we cope with the loss? Aunt Alice was tired, but it was hard for her to sleep because she kept thinking of people she ought to call, and she didn't want to miss any of the friends who came to visit. At the end of a long day, she said quietly, "I have so much to be thankful for. Sam and I were married for sixty years. He was a good man. I prayed that God would take him gently, and he did. I'm going to miss him, but I don't feel bad he's gone." She did "not grieve as others do who have no hope" (1 Thessalonians 4:13).

It's never easy to say good-bye to someone we love, and it's especially hard when he or she seems too young. I received the word early one morning in Munich that my sixteen-year-old brother Benjamin had been killed instantly in a car crash in Georgia. Three months earlier, my husband and I had said good-bye to our families before flying to Germany to live for three years. How could we have known that the farewell picnic snapshots were the last we'd take of Ben?

I couldn't be there with my family, but we talked together on the phone. Both Mother and Daddy comforted me, reminding me that Ben's life had been an affirmation of Paul's words: "For to me to live is Christ, and to die is gain" (Philippians 1:21). From a neighborhood flower shop, I ordered a fiery red azalea plant to be delivered with this card, "He lives and sings praises to our God."

When we are the ones planning a service for a saint who is with God, if we reflect that hope in the memorial service, we are honoring the person by honoring his God. Yes, there will be many words about the one who's gone. But may our songs and eulogies and homilies be filled with God, so that as we remember our loved one, we can paraphrase 1 Peter 1:3-5:

> Blessed be the God and Father of our Lord Jesus Christ! According to his great mercy, he has caused [_____] to be born again to a living hope through the resurrection of Jesus Christ from the dead, to an inheritance that is imperishable, undefiled, and unfading, kept in heaven for [_____], who by God's power [was] guarded through faith for a salvation ready to be revealed in the last time.

THANKSGIVING DAY

What more could we ask for than that hope and salvation? "Blessed be the God and Father of our Lord Jesus Christ!" (1 Peter 1:3). Sometimes we can't help pouring out our praise and thanks to God—which brings us to Thanksgiving Day.

What are the requirements for any sort of thanksgiving to happen? Something we're thankful for and somebody to thank. Seems so obvious, but I think I need to say it because it's amazing how many people can say, "I'm thankful for . . ." without admitting that God is there to hear their thanks. And they're certainly not giving him credit for whatever it is they're enjoying.

So what turns the fourth Thursday of November into Thanksgiving? Turkey? I know one family who doesn't like turkey. Their traditional Thanksgiving meal is Vietnamese carryout. But whatever our food traditions, is that all there is? Not if we plan *real* thanks into the day.

Maybe we can start by giving someone else a reason to give thanks. It might be by food donations we make ahead of time. It might be through invitations to our table—someone with no relatives nearby, a newly-arrived refugee family, a lonely neighbor.

And then how will we express our thanks to God? Perhaps there's a poster on the wall where anyone during the day can write or draw pictures of what he or she is thanking God for. Perhaps one of the children will make place cards with a verse of thanks on each, to be read sometime during the meal. Maybe this is a good day to pull out the year's journals or photo albums or videos to remind each other of all that God has done in our lives this year. And maybe Dad will begin the meal by reading or singing some words from Scripture, such as Psalm 95 below.

> *1Oh come, let us sing to the LORD;*
> *let us make a joyful noise to the rock of our salvation!*
> *2Let us come into his presence with thanksgiving;*
> *let us make a joyful noise to him with songs of praise!*
> *3For the LORD is a great God, and a great King above all gods. . . .*
> *6Oh come, let us worship and bow down;*
> *let us kneel before the LORD, our Maker!*
> *7For he is our God, and we are the people of his pasture,*
> *and the sheep of his hand.*
>
> (PSALM 95:1-3, 6-7)

"The people of his pasture, and the sheep of his hand. . . ." Our Shepherd knows we need "especially" occasions to round up our attention and direct our thoughts toward him.

Oh, save your people and
bless your heritage!
Be their shepherd and carry them forever.
(PSALM 28:9)

Imogene had the baby doll but she wasn't carrying it in the way she was supposed to, cradled in her arms. She had it slung up over her shoulder, and before she put it in the manger she thumped it twice on the back.

I heard Alice gasp and she poked me. "I don't think it's very nice to burp the baby Jesus," she whispered, "as if he had colic." Then she poked me again. "Do you suppose he could have had colic?"

I said, "I don't know why not," and I didn't. He could have had colic, or been fussy, or hungry like any other baby. After all, that was the whole point of Jesus—that he didn't come down on a cloud like something out of "Amazing Comics," but that he was born and lived . . . a real person.

BARBARA ROBINSON
The Best Christmas Pageant Ever[9]

EIGHT

ESPECIALLY CHRISTMAS

Why in the world would God send his Son among us as a *baby?* Just think of almighty God waving his arms and legs and lying in place until someone decided to pick him up, getting hungrier until somebody decided to feed him, remaining dirty until someone cleaned and changed him. This is not reasonable—not by our standards, that is. But God has his own purposes. Perhaps one reason for God becoming a baby is that so many people desire a baby, love children, and suffer until a child arrives. God uses that yearning to draw us toward his Son, Jesus.

Christmas is only one small part of a whole year of living, working, and ministering in our churches and to our neighbors, of meeting our family's physical needs, of teaching our children. Just one small part of the year—but with our hearts and spirits open in anticipation and excitement, what an ideal opportunity for remembering and teaching.

We've seen in earlier chapters how important it is to *plan* our "everyday" traditions so that we reflect our view of the world and God. How much more important our planning is for celebrations of a world-shaking event like God being born a baby so that we can be reborn as his children.

ADVENT

We are a people of promise. For centuries God prepared people for the coming of his Son, our only hope for life. At Christmas we celebrate the fulfillment of the promises God made—that he would make a way to draw near to him.

Advent is what we call the season leading up to Christmas. It begins four Sundays before December 25, sometimes in the last weekend of November, sometimes on the first Sunday in December.

> I PETER 1:10-12
> 10Concerning this salvation, the prophets who prophesied about the grace that was to be yours searched and inquired carefully, 11inquiring what person or time the Spirit of Christ in them was indicating when he predicted the sufferings of Christ and the subsequent glories. 12It was revealed to them that they were serving not themselves but you, in the things that have now been announced to you through those who preached the good news to you by the Holy Spirit sent from heaven, things into which angels long to look.

First Peter 1:10-12 is a clear description of what we look back to during Advent. For four weeks, it's as if we're reenacting, remembering the thousands of years during which God's people were anticipating and longing for the coming of God's salvation, for Jesus. That's what advent means—"coming." Even God's men who foretold the grace that was to come didn't know "what person or time the Spirit of Christ in them was indicating" (v. 11). They were waiting, but they didn't know what God's salvation would look like.

In fact, God revealed to them that they were not the ones who would see the sufferings and glory of God's Christ. "They were serving not themselves but you, in the things that have now been announced to you through those who preached the good news to you by the Holy Spirit sent from heaven" (v. 12). They were serving us. We

Christians on this side of Jesus' birth are a God-blessed, happy people because we know God's plan. The centuries of waiting are over. We have the greatest reason to celebrate.

And yet we are still waiting. Our spiritual redemption came to us with the baby of Bethlehem. Nonetheless, as Romans 8 says, "we ourselves, who have the firstfruits of the Spirit, groan inwardly as we wait eagerly for adoption as sons, the redemption of our bodies" (v. 23). There is suffering and tragedy still, even for Christians. Someone we love is dying. We may be in pain. Sometimes we have trouble believing God's promises. In other words, our redemption is not complete. We are waiting for the redemption of our bodies—waiting for Jesus' second advent, for him to come again.

So here we stand in the middle. Advent is a season of looking back, thinking how it must have been, waiting for the promised salvation of God, not knowing what to expect. And at the same time, Advent is a season of looking ahead, preparing ourselves to meet Jesus at his Second Coming.

ADVENT—LOOKING BACK

Probably the two most common symbols of Advent are candles or a calendar. That's appropriate, since each is a way of waiting for Christmas.

Advent Candles

Various helpful schemes of symbolism can be attached to the candles, their number, and color. But here are the basics—one candle for each of the Sundays of Advent and, if you wish, a fifth for Christmas Day. On the first Sunday, only one candle will be lit, then two on the second Sunday, and so forth. That's all that's *necessary*. But if we want our Advent candles to be more than a centerpiece, we have to ask ourselves, "What makes these more than wax and wick?"

The flame is a symbol of the one who is called "the light of the world." We who follow him "will not walk in darkness, but will have the light of life" (John 8:12). As we move closer to the day when we'll meet him, there is greater and greater brightness.

JOHN 8:12
Jesus spoke to them, saying, "I am the light of the world. Whoever follows me will not walk in darkness, but will have the light of life."

But we need to remember that our very young children will see only candles. No matter how much we explain the symbolism, they need some more years before they can comprehend the meaning of the candles. That's why I always incorporate a manger scene into our Advent candle arrangement. *Tangible* is my guiding word. What a child can see and touch, he might understand a little more clearly. Tangible things help us adults as well.

Each Advent Sunday, we Pipers gather at the table for a meal and hear a word from the Bible before lighting the next candle. When the children were younger, each week's passage probably would be one part of the Christmas story from Matthew or Luke. As they've grown older, we've expanded the reading to include Old Testament prophecies of the Messiah's coming. Then on other days, whenever we sit at the dining room table where the candles are the centerpiece, we light that week's number of candles.

The light, brighter by the week, points us toward Jesus who has called us to be "a chosen race, a royal priesthood, a holy nation, a people for his own possession, that [we] may proclaim the excellencies of him who called [us] out of darkness into his marvelous light" (1 Peter 2:9).

Advent Calendar

"Mommy, Mommy! May I open the next window on the calendar?" A simple pasteboard Advent calendar with one flap to open on each day in December is probably the most familiar way to help a child understand the wait until Christmas. In the stores several themes are likely to be available, including Swiss mountain villages and Santa's workshops. But since the Advent—the coming—we're waiting for is Christ's, let's make sure our daily countdown has a real *Christ*mas setting.

For our family a more permanent calendar has become a tradition. When our first child was a toddler, I could find hardly any Christmas things that had to do with Jesus. So I created the Noël Calendar, a burlap banner with plastic and wood figures that by December 25 have been attached with Velcro across the top half of the banner to represent the Christmas story. Throughout the month, that story is told in increments, starting over at the beginning and adding a bit more each day.[10]

The first year we used the calendar, I learned an important lesson: Repetition is an excellent way for a child to memorize. In mid-December, when Karsten was barely two, my mother-in-law died in a bus crash in Israel. With little time to plan, we were on our way from Minnesota to South Carolina to take care of my father-in-law, who had been injured. On an impulse I had tossed the calendar into a suitcase. In the midst of so much confusion, shock, and irregularity, Karsten forgot everything he'd learned about potty training and too much of what he knew about behaving. But even though he could hardly make a whole sentence on his own yet, he could pick up the Christmas story at any point and keep it going, word for word, as he'd heard it day after day when we did the calendar.

In chapter 4 of this book we thought about the importance of repetition and regularity. This period in Karsten's life was the time when I began to realize the place of these things in my life with my children—repeating regularly the story that for centuries God's people had longed to know.

ADVENT—LOOKING FORWARD

The verses we read earlier from 1 Peter 1 (vv. 10-12, p. 76) look backward toward God's people who were awaiting his salvation. The very next verses look forward in Advent, anticipating the return of Jesus. "Therefore, preparing your minds for action, and being sober-minded, set your hope fully on the grace that will be brought to you at the revelation of Jesus Christ" (v. 13). There will be another advent of Christ; he will come again.

Advent is a season for introspection. Peter gives us God's high standard as we contemplate our standing with him: "You shall be holy, for I am holy" (v. 16). This is a time to ask ourselves questions:

> **1 PETER 1:13-19**
> 13Therefore, preparing your minds for action, and being sober-minded, set your hope fully on the grace that will be brought to you at the revelation of Jesus Christ. 14As obedient children, do not be conformed to the passions of your former ignorance, 15but as he who called you is holy, you also be holy in all your conduct, 16since it is written, "You shall be holy, for I am holy." 17And if you call on him as Father who judges impartially according to each one's deeds, conduct yourselves with fear throughout the time of your exile, 18knowing that you were ransomed from the futile ways inherited from your forefathers, not with perishable things such as silver or gold, 19but with the precious blood of Christ, like that of a lamb without blemish or spot.

- Am I clear-thinking and sober-minded, or are my concerns mainly trivial? (v. 13)
- Is my hope set fully on the grace I will receive from Jesus at his Second Coming, or do I cringe at the thought of leaving behind the life I love? (v. 13)
- Am I an obedient child of my Father, or am I still shaped by the passions that drove me before I became a Christian? (v. 14)

If regular personal devotions are not part of our lives, Advent would be a time tailor-made to begin. We remember that God charged the adults in Deuteronomy 11 to "lay up these words of mine in *your* heart and in *your* soul" (v. 18, emphasis mine), and that he expects us to "love the LORD [our] God" (v. 1). The living water in our own hearts is the fountain from which we shower Christ on our family. Our time with God and his preparation of us is a necessary foundation. Without it our Christmas activities will degenerate into hoopla.

But however much we want a significant Christmas celebration for our families, that is not the primary reason for our contemplation and self-examination. Our deeper motivation is the strengthening of our ultimate hope in Jesus, "so that when he appears we may have confidence and not shrink from him in shame at his coming" (1 John 2:28).

May this time be a reflection of what our lives are—gratitude for the promises that were fulfilled when God gave us the gift of his Son and anticipation of and preparation for Christ's coming again.

Do Others See Why We Celebrate?

How will our home look if our celebration is a picture of anticipation and waiting for God's plan to be completed, a picture of our joy in the salvation he has begun for us? What visible things will fill our house as we celebrate what God has done through Jesus?

Thinking About Santa

For several reasons, we have chosen not to include Santa Claus in our Christmas stories and decorations. First, fairy tales are fun, but we don't ask our children to believe them. Second, celebrating with Santa *and* manger will postpone a child's clear understanding of what the real truth of God is. It's very difficult for a young child to pick through a marble cake of part truth and part imagination to find the crumbs of reality. We want our children to understand God as fully as they're able, at whatever age they are. So we try to avoid anything that would inhibit or distort that understanding.

Third, think how confusing it must be to a literal-thinking, uncritical preschooler. Santa is so much like what we're trying all year to teach our children about God. Look at the "attributes" of Santa:

- He's omniscient—he sees everything you do.
- He rewards you if you're good.
- He's omnipresent—at least, he can be everywhere in one night.
- He gives you good gifts.
- He's the most famous "old man in the sky" figure.

But at the deeper level that young children can't comprehend yet, he is not like God at all. For example, does Santa really care if we're bad or good? Think of the most awful kid you can remember. Did he or she ever *not* get gifts from Santa? What about Santa's spying and then rewarding you if you're good enough? That's not the way God operates. He gave us his gift—his Son—even though we weren't good at all. "God shows his love for us in that while we were still sinners, Christ died for us" (Romans 5:8). He gave his gift to us to make us good, not because we had proved ourselves good enough.

Helping our children understand God as much as they're able at whatever age they are is our primary goal. But we've also seen some other encouraging effects of not including Santa in our celebration.

First, I think children are glad to realize that their parents, who live with them all year and know all the worst things about them, still show their love at Christmas. Isn't that better than a funny, old make-believe man who drops in just once a year?

Second, our children know our family's usual giving patterns for birthdays and special events. They seem to have an instinct about our typical spending levels and abilities. Knowing that their Christmas gifts come from the people they love, rather than from a bottomless sack, can help diminish the "I-want-this, give-me-that" syndrome.

And, finally, when children know that God's generosity is reflected by God's people, it tends to encourage a sense of responsibility about helping make Christmas good for others.

Karsten, for example, worked hard on one gift one year. On Christmas morning in 1975, my husband stepped around a large, loose-flapped cardboard box to get to his chair at the breakfast table. "Where's Karsten?" he asked, expecting to see our excited three-year-old raring to leap into the day.

Sitting down, I said, "He'll be here in a minute." I nudged the box with my toe.

Karsten threw back the flaps and rose to his full three-foot stature. "And there were shepherds living out in the fields nearby, keeping watch over their flocks at night. An angel of the Lord appeared to them . . ." He had memorized Luke 2:8-20 as a gift for his dad. Karsten knew Santa wasn't the one to depend on.

In fact, a few days later Karsten and I were walking down the hall at church. One of the older ladies leaned down to squeeze his pink, round cheek and asked, "What did Santa bring you?"

Karsten's head jerked quickly toward me, and he whispered loudly, "Doesn't she know?"

These thoughts raise the question: If not Santa, then what?

Manger Scenes

Our very first Christmas was in the middle of our honeymoon. So our traditions began the second year of marriage. We visited our families before Christmas and returned to our small place late at night on December 21. We didn't have any decorations, and the time was short. So we decided not to buy a tree. I had found a tiny nativity set at an international gift shop. On Christmas morning, the two of us sat on the floor beside a low, small table with that scene between us. Christmas carols played in the background as we opened each other's gifts. It seemed exactly right that Jesus be the visible center.

So every year since then, a special crèche has been the focal point of our celebration. We arrange it on a table and collect our gifts underneath. This is often the gathering place for our family devotions during December. Anyone who visits sees what our center is.

We also use a manger scene as part of our Advent candle arrangement to keep the focus of our waiting visible before us. Other uses for a crèche might be:

- An unbreakable set for the children to play with.
- Manger scene ornaments for the Christmas tree.
- A stained-glass or colored-cellophane window arrangement visible from the street.
- A play corner with toy lamb, baby doll, and appropriate items for costumes.

One friend told me about her crèche collection:

I try to find one in every place I visit. I give traveling friends $20 to spend on a nativity for me if they happen to see one where they are going. I find them at garage sales and thrift stores and after-Christmas sales, and people give them to me as gifts. I have more than a hundred now from all over the world, and when I get them out for Christmas, it is a wonderful reminder that one day people from all tribes and tongues and people and languages—not just my own country—will worship the King.

Other Symbols

One year I read through the Bible looking for names of God and word pictures that describe him. I filled every flyleaf, listing them for Father, Son, and Holy Spirit.[11] Each name or image is a facet of the God who is too complex and deep for us to ever know completely. But as we gaze at him from one angle and then from another, we see more clearly the whole, complete, perfect person he is. And the more we know him, the more we love him.

There is no other time in our year set aside to think so happily and thoroughly about who Jesus is and what he's done. That makes Advent and Christmas a perfect time to put in front of us everything we can think of that reminds us of him.

While the children are very young, one way to create visual reminders is by using a large bare branch as a Bethlehem Tree. It would be hung with ornaments and items that picture or symbolize the Bethlehem event.

When children are older, the branch might become a Jesus Tree, reaching further for its symbolism, to include:

- Ornaments and items that represent the nativity.
- Items that relate to Jesus' life.
- Symbols of who Jesus is, as found in Scripture's names for him, word pictures, and parables.
- Reminders of Old Testament prophecy and history leading up to his birth.

A FEW REMINDERS OF JESUS' LIFE
Star, stable, holy family, Wise Men, and other nativity symbols
Shepherd (nativity visitors; he is the Good Shepherd)
Toy hammer, saw (he was a carpenter)
Nails (carpenter; crucifixion)
Grapes (Last Supper)
Praying hands
Thorns
Cross

A FEW SYMBOLS OF PROPHECY AND HISTORY
Bible, scroll
Wheat (his ancestor Ruth; Bread of Life)
Heart (God so loved the world)
Joseph's coat, Noah's Ark (God saving his people)
Church

WORD PICTURES AND NAMES OF JESUS
Lion (of Judah)
Rose (of Sharon)
Sun (of righteousness)
Sheep (Lamb of God)
Globe (he takes away the sin of the world)
Crown (eternal King)
Dove (Prince of Peace; he left his Spirit with us)
Candle (Light of the World)

Many of our Jesus Tree items are not "ornaments." They are made of cloth or sticks or clay, or we reinvented something as a symbol. For example, the lion is from an old zoo game; the hammer and saw were part of a toddler's tool set; the globe is a key ring.

The facets of Jesus are even more significant to us if we discover them ourselves. Perhaps our Jesus Tree preparations and our Advent spiritual preparation can mesh as we read the Gospels, say, trying to find out who Jesus is.

AM I REFLECTING GOD'S GENEROSITY?

Just about everything in our culture is commercialized. So why does it bother us so much to see Christmas taken over as a sales opportunity? Isn't it because the eagerness to make money off Jesus' birth is the very opposite of God's action in giving

IMAGINARY LETTER TO BEIJING
(Based on a real visitor's questions about our child's manger scene)

December 26

Dear Mother,

I am working diligently in my university courses, and usually I understand the English fairly easily. But I am glad to write to you in Chinese. Thank you again for allowing me this opportunity to study in the United States.

I hope you are well. I am fine, but there is so much to learn about a new place. October 1, as you have taught me well, is the proper day to begin wearing long underwear again. Imagine my embarrassment at the jocular comments of my dorm companions when they saw my attire. In America they pay no attention to the appropriate dress for the date. Rather, if it grows cool so early in the season, they turn on the central heating, not waiting for the designated fire-up-the-furnace day!

I have heard much about the American holiday, Christmas, and so I was eager to find out more about it now that I am here. One realizes the importance of the festival when one sees its trappings in public more than two months before its actual date of December 25. I will tell you some of what I have seen, although it is difficult to interpret the true function of each element.

One first notices the miles-long strings of tiny lights draped over houses, businesses, and trees. Since this is the darkest time of the year, perhaps they are part of some ancient winter solstice ritual ("ancient" by American standards, that is).

I have seen many forms of greenery—juniper, fir, pine, holly, mistletoe. There may be some fine distinction between one and another. I am not sure. But the lush mistletoe seems to have some connection with an "ancient" courting or fertility ceremony.

By far, the most pervasive symbol of Christmas is a character called "Santa Claus," a rotund, cheerful, red-suited, white-bearded, larger-than-life being. He is often seen surrounded by miniature creatures somewhat like himself, called elves. Sometimes he is portrayed waving from a reindeer-drawn snow vehicle, positioned as if it were flying. Often also there are glittery "icicles," aerosol spray-on "snow," and snowflake ornaments, leading one to suspect that Christmas might be a celebration of winter, with

Santa Claus somehow as its personification. I see him everywhere, and so I had been thinking he must be the key to Christmas if one could only delve deeply enough into the mystery.

Then I received an unexpected invitation to visit an American family on Christmas afternoon. At last! I thought. An opportunity to see firsthand a genuine observance. Imagine my dismay yesterday when all my previous assumptions were shattered. There was not one hint of Santa Claus anywhere in this home even though there were several children. (I had assumed that Santa Claus was considered especially valuable for instructing children in the "ancient" truths.)

What did I see instead? Tiny cowsheds filled with toy-sized animals and people. What relation did these bear to any of the Christmas symbolism I had observed in past weeks? Not wanting to appear foolish, I waited until a moment arrived when all of the adults were out of the room. Then I leaned over to a small son of the home, gestured toward a cowshed, and inquired softly, "What is that?"

For an instant, he looked surprised, and I feared I would be shamed by a mere child's recognition of my ignorance. But almost immediately, his face lit with liveliness as he began to recount a story—a story whose details he seemed to know intimately, young as he was.

He spoke of a stable and a baby, of angels and shepherds, and of a star and wise men. When his parents returned to the room, I wasn't finished listening, and I had forgotten about looking foolish. So I asked them for more. Their story started with a serpent, sin, futility, and despair and ended with God's Son, the Savior who gives hope and a future, and with God and his glory. They say this baby is God. Can this be?

Dear Mother, it is late. Though there is much more to write, I must continue another time. But, Mother, is it possible? Could it be that I have found the most ancient— the truly most ancient—mystery?

Your wondering son

him? God pours out his riches on us. He even gave us the life and death of his beloved Son. How do we show that we are children of that generous Father?

We will find our own ways, not by the size of our gifts, but by our choices of gift recipients, of guests in our home, and of the kinds of presents we give.

Gift to Jesus

It may be easy for us to forget that this is Jesus' *birthday.* That usually means gifts to the birthday person. Children especially will think it normal that Jesus should receive something for his birthday. We'll need to talk with them about what it means to give a gift to Jesus since we can't put it in his hand. One of the unusual things about Jesus is that when we give a gift to him, other people benefit. "And the King will answer them, 'Truly, I say to you, as you did it to one of the least of these my brothers, you did it to me'" (Matthew 25:40).

If you decide early in the Advent season where your gift is going, you can be praying for the recipient throughout the season. Your prayer becomes an added gift to the family with special needs, the Christian relief agency, the local ministry, the missionary, or whomever you have chosen.

Money isn't the only thing we can give, but for the moment, let's think about financial gifts. How might you decide on the amount? One possibility is to determine what percentage of your total gift expenditures will be set aside for Jesus. Another is to give him your December coffee break money or some other regular expenditure.

What about our children? Some years I have offered "wages" for special jobs or even for regular chores during December, with the understanding that this money is being earned for Jesus' gift.

Shepherd's Pouch

The children at our house have had a simple drawstring bag—a shepherd's pouch, we call it—in which to collect Jesus' gift throughout December. On Christmas Eve, during a special family worship time, the children lay their pouches beside the manger of our special nativity scene. We speak to them then of giving their gifts to Jesus, as the shepherds came, giving Jesus worship and wonder.

When the angels went away from them into heaven, the shepherds said to one another, "Let us go over to Bethlehem and see this thing that has happened, which the Lord has made known to us." And they went with haste and found Mary and Joseph, and the baby lying in a manger. And when they saw it, they made known the saying that had been told them concerning this child. And all who heard it won-

dered at what the shepherds told them. . . . And the shepherds returned, glorifying
and praising God for all they had heard and seen, as it had been told them.

(LUKE 2: 15-20)

On Christmas morning, the coins have been removed and added to our grown-up gifts, ready to be sent to our chosen recipient. And the children find in their pouches several small gifts. We speak of a God who blesses those who love and trust him. Although these particular tokens are tangible and physical, our children know from our lifestyle and teaching throughout the year that God blesses in many ways. In fact, many people who are most blessed have very little visible wealth. The blessing of God is his presence with us, which gives us constant cause for praise.

Because your steadfast love is better than life,
my lips will praise you.
So I will bless you as long as I live;
in your name I will lift up my hands.
My soul will be satisfied as with fat and rich food,
and my mouth will praise you with joyful lips,
when I remember you upon my bed,
and meditate on you in the watches of the night;
for you have been my help,
and in the shadow of your wings I will sing for joy.
My soul clings to you;
your right hand upholds me.

(PSALM 63:3-8)

Perhaps the following questions can help us prepare for Christmas.

- Am I my Father's child? Do I resemble him in my generosity?
- Am I focusing on God's gift so that my appreciation to him grows?
- Can others see why I am celebrating?
- Am I celebrating Christ?

One November a friend of mine almost lost her child. By Christmas the crisis was past, but they still were not sure of the long-term implications. She e-mailed me during the season that had always been her favorite time of the year:

Surprisingly, I'm finding Christmas hard. A little bit I resent all the hoopla; sometimes I want to shout, "Don't you know my baby could have died?" At the same time I'm very grateful she's alive, and very aware that she might not have been. So you'd think I'd be really, really happy! That's a pretty secular statement. In spiritual terms, Christmas is not very meaningful to me this year one way or the other. I feel a bit like God and I are on a journey together, seeing and doing a lot, but certainly not staying anywhere for any length of time.

My answer to her could well be the summary of this chapter:

It's not at all surprising that Christmas is hard for you this year. The reason for Christmas is the same as it ever was, and nothing is more essential to our lives than the Incarnation. What's different for you, I expect, is that the traditions we wrap around December 25 to make it different from other days, those traditions and activities are as nothing to you this year. In fact, the thought of them probably weighs like a lump of lead in your belly. So what! Trees are nothing. Feasts are nothing. Lights are nothing. Music is nothing.

Only Christ matters. He is the only reason that you can be on any sort of journey with God, that you can have anything at all to do with God. Only Jesus matters. Hold on to that. Even if your little girl had not survived. But she did, praise Jesus!

One time I told someone in hard times, "Just hang in there." But she corrected me, "I'm not just hanging in there. I'm trying to hang on to Jesus."

So, please, just keep hanging on to Jesus.

Sometimes, when things are going well, we might too easily forget that we have only one sure, immovable, dependable strength—Jesus, who was a baby once and is always and forever God. That is what holds us and keeps us whether or not we can carry out our traditions. May our decorations, gifts, and festivities—or lack of them—never block our view of him but always point us toward him.

Only Christ matters.

hol·i·day
Etymology: Middle English, from Old English halig, holy + dæg, day; holy day, day set aside for special religious observance

crux
Etymology: Latin cruc-, crux, cross
1. an essential point requiring resolution or resolving an outcome
2. a main or central feature

cru·cial
Etymology: Latin cruc-, crux, cross important or essential as resolving a crisis, decisive

NINE

ESPECIALLY EASTER

Growing up in the South at a time when there was a lot more etiquette in the air, I learned an important lesson about Easter: That's the day you can begin to wear white shoes again after winter. Fortunately, my family and church taught me more *crucial* lessons about the *holiday* that marks the *crux* of the Christian's life.

Crucial, crux, holiday—in these words we see even our language bowing to the essential nature of the event we remember during Lent and Easter. Good Friday is not just a day off work; it is a holy day. Easter's Resurrection could happen only after the Crucifixion, and the cross is like a crossroads in our lives. Every one of us must stand at that crux, that point requiring resolution, and must choose which way to go. The decision we make is crucial—the crisis of our lives is resolved by our turn toward either life or death. Jesus said, "Truly, truly, I say to you, whoever hears my word and believes him who sent me has eternal life. He does not come into judgment, but has passed from death to life" (John 5:24).

We reveal to ourselves and others what is important to us by the way we celebrate. Is the season before Easter mainly a hassle to get to the mall and a strain on the budget purchasing clothes, candy, cards, and groceries for a big dinner? Or is it several days or weeks of considering God's work in our lives through Jesus, along with special activities to help us think about Jesus' death and resurrection?

Over the course of the Lenten and Easter season, we are remembering the lowest points of sin and the highest peaks of what God has done for us through Jesus. We have a way, the only way, to the Father through Jesus. That's worth celebrating!

Jesus said . . . , "I am the way, and the truth, and the life. No one comes to the Father except through me."

(JOHN 14:6)

For God so loved the world, that he gave his only Son, that whoever believes in him should not perish but have eternal life.

(JOHN 3:16)

And yet every year somehow it's so easy for Easter to slip up on us, and suddenly we're saying, "Oh, my goodness, it's Palm Sunday already!" Let's think of some ways to be prepared, to be waiting for Easter.

Although Easter is the highest celebration of the Christian year, it doesn't have the fascination and thrill that surrounds Christmas. There's a reason: The death of Jesus was a very somber and tragic event, and we had a part in causing it. But we mustn't avoid preparation for Easter simply because the sober, contemplative season of Lent precedes it. As with all the other special times of our year, we'll be wise and obedient if we start by preparing our own hearts and lives. Lent offers us seven weeks for this purpose.

LENT

Lent comes from an Old English word that means *lengthen,* signifying that the days are getting longer because spring is here. Among many Christians Lent has come to mean the pre-Easter season that begins on Ash Wednesday.

Traditionally Lent is a season of sober, realistic reflection on our own lives and our need for a Savior. It is a time for turning away from anything that has kept us from God and for turning or returning to him. It is a time to pray that God will renew our love for him and our dependence on him.

FASTING

In some churches, fasting has been a traditional way of expressing dependence on God during Lent. Of course, like any other religious observance, fasting is only as significant as the intent of the heart. The practice may be nothing more than legalism, or on the other hand, it can be a way of saying, "Oh, God, I want you more than I want any of the good things in my life—food, videos, crossword puzzles, shopping, etc. You are the one who fulfills my desires."

We may find that a fast of some sort helps us recognize our reliance on God. Whether it's a fast from some particular food or meal or from some activity, such as watching TV, reading the newspaper, or surfing the Web, we need to remember that fasting is two-sided. It's not just turning away from something for a while, but it is also turning toward God. In the time that is "added" to our day through fasting from some activity, we might:

- consider the depth of our sin and the height of God's love in Jesus, asking God for forgiveness.
- remember Jesus' forty days of fasting and temptation in the wilderness, and consider the temptations that hit us the hardest.
- pray for our enemies and the people in our lives who are most difficult to like.
- pray for the salvation of a neighbor, coworker, or family member.

> FASTING
>
> Christian fasting is a test to see what desires control us.
>
> Fasting reveals the measure of food's mastery over us—or television or computers or whatever we submit to again and again to conceal the weakness of our hunger for God.
>
> A real lived-out human act of preference for God over his gifts is the actual lived-out glorification of God's excellence for which he created the world. Fasting is not the only way, or the main way, that we glorify God in preferring him above his gifts. But it is one way.
>
> JOHN PIPER
> *A Hunger for God* 12

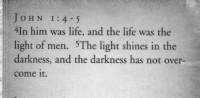

One thing we have tried to do in our family is "fast" during Holy Week from entertainment and activities that are not in the same spirit as the commemorations of Maundy Thursday, Good Friday, and the "waiting" Saturday that follows those tragic days. If we owned a television, I expect we'd cut way back or simply unplug it. We're not likely to go to a movie or a party, and we try to save any kid's overnight visits with friends till later.

Even if we don't feel led to fast during Lent, let's ask God to show us what it is that we depend too much on, and ask him to help us cut back that dependence while we lean all the more on him.

LENTEN CANDLES

Lent is a season of waiting. In that sense it is like Advent. But while Advent waits eagerly for the appearance of the Savior, Lent waits, with heavy responsibility, for his death. The light of the Advent candles grows brighter as we approach the Savior's arrival. In Lent all grows darker as we draw nearer to the unthinkable—the death of God.

To symbolize this, we can begin Lent with seven lighted candles. On the first Sunday, one is snuffed out. On the second Sunday, the second candle is extinguished, and so on until Good Friday, when the last one is darkened. It is as if we have seen sin growing in power and finally crucifying the Light of the World, leaving us in darkness.

But John 1:5 assures us, "The light shines in the darkness, and the darkness has not overcome it." On Easter morning, all the candles shine triumphantly. The darkness *cannot* put out the Light.[13]

RESURRECTION TREE

At our house during Advent, before Christmas we decorate a Jesus Tree with everything we can think of that reminds us of who Jesus is, of his earthly life and ancestors, and of prophecies concerning him. In January we store away all those symbols in the attic, except the ones related to the Crucifixion and Resurrection. When Lent arrives, we use these familiar items on our Resurrection Tree. They become a tangible representation of the connection between Christmas and Easter, the two anchors of a Christian's year.

The Resurrection Tree is a bare branch, broken from a bush in the back yard, just as the Jesus Tree was. On its twigs we hang symbols that remind us of the Crucifixion and Resurrection and things that point us toward the names and facets of Jesus that are related especially to his sacrifice for our redemption.

As at Advent, the symbols we place before us will have deeper meaning if we have "found" them ourselves. Perhaps those discoveries will occur as we consider the state of our relationship with Jesus and our understanding of the salvation he offers us. Reading the gospel accounts of his last days (Matthew 21—28; Mark 11—16; Luke 19—24; John 11—21) will be essential for this consideration. Like the symbols on Advent's Jesus Tree, most of these objects won't be ornaments but small toys and household items that we "re-create."

HOLY WEEK

If the children in your life are young, Lent may be too long a waiting time. In that case, the week that begins with Palm Sunday may

be just long enough for anticipating Easter. At our house, we use a play dough mountain and chenille stick (pipe cleaner) people to depict what happened during the week.

As you're reading in the Gospels, make a list of the days beginning with Palm Sunday and ending with Easter. Try to assign parts of the Holy Week story to each day. I realize that it's not clear on which day some things happened, but spread out the events in order as evenly as you can.

Each day we play out part of the story with the chenille stick people. Finally on Good Friday the Jesus figure is placed on the cross and then laid in the grave under the mountain with a rock "sealing" the entrance. After activity all week, there is nothing to do on Saturday except wait. Perhaps that gives the children a tiny bit of empathy for the disciples who were hidden away, thinking all was lost.

Making an Easter Mountain

Play Dough

4 c. flour	1 1/2 c. water
1 1/2 c. salt	1 Tbs. oil

Mix ingredients and knead. Add small amounts of water as needed until the texture is right.

Mountain

1. Use two backyard sticks bound together with twine to make a cross about five or six inches tall.

2. Shape the whole lump of play dough into a mountain. The size will be determined by the volume of your play dough. Leave an opening on one side into the "cave" that will represent the tomb, using your fist or a soup can to hold the space open.

3. Press the cross into the top of the mountain to form a hole deep enough to stand the cross in. Make the hole a bit larger than the actual stick circumference because the hole will get smaller as the mountain bakes. Set the cross aside.

4. Twist toothpicks into the dough or press fork tines randomly around on the hill to make "footholds" for chenille stick people.

5. Press the rock that will cover the tomb against the opening, to shape a better fit. Set the stone aside.

6. Bake at 250° for four to five hours. When cooled, color as desired with paint or markers.

The first year we made an Easter mountain, three-year-old Karsten woke on Easter morning and pattered out to the dining room to check the mountain. He saw "Jesus" astride the top of the hill, arms raised in triumph. After a few motionless moments of silence, Karsten shouted, "He's alive! Jesus is alive!"

This activity is excellent for as many years as children can enjoy it and take it somewhat seriously. As soon as it starts to be treated as silly, it's time to set it aside. The reality of the Crucifixion is too deep and horrendous to be treated lightly.

I felt the weight of it most heavily, I think, as I watched a video brought home by a missionary from a nation where it is very difficult to be a Christian—where many people have suffered for their faith. We watched as the brothers and sisters in a house church broke bread together in remembrance of Jesus' death. Their tears and cries and spasms of grief were so overwhelming they could hardly eat and drink. It was as if Jesus were being crucified before them at that very moment.

It is no small thing to "proclaim the Lord's death" (1 Corinthians 11:26), which is what we are doing not just on Good Friday, but every time we eat and drink together the Lord's Supper. Jesus' suffering is very real to his people who suffer because of their faith. May we not take our Lord's death for granted. Our lives depend on it.

I don't want to aim so purposefully toward Easter that I speed unthinkingly past the cross. But at the same time, the Crucifixion—Jesus' death—is not the end.

EASTER

After the somber days of Lent, we wake to Easter morning. At our house that means I slip downstairs ahead of the children to set out the breakfast cake and turn on some "hallelujah music" to meet the family as they appear. A lamb cake, representing the Lamb of God, decorates the table and will be dessert later in the day. All the Lenten candles burn brightly because the Light of the World has overcome the darkness. At the table together we read the story of the Resurrection.

Then—the high point of the day—we gather with other glad believers to worship our *living* God and cry together, "The Lord is risen! The Lord is risen indeed!" This is the cry that resonates through *all* our celebrations and traditions through all the year. If it were not so, it wouldn't matter what our traditions were or even if we had any. If it were not so, we would have no eternal inheritance, no Heirloom that is God himself.

Blessed be the God and Father of our Lord Jesus Christ! According to his great mercy, he has caused us to be born again to a living hope through the resurrection of Jesus Christ from the dead, to an inheritance that is imperishable, undefiled, and unfading, kept in heaven for you, who by God's power are being guarded through faith for a salvation ready to be revealed in the last time.

(1 Peter 1:3-5)

Other Lenten and Easter Ideas

- Pull out all your CDs or tapes of Easter music. Have them handy to pop into your player.
- Read books that will deepen your spiritual life and your understanding of what God has done. Ideas might include missionary biographies or *The Pleasures of God* (John Piper), in particular the chapter entitled "God's Pleasure in Bruising His Son." You could use *The Man Born to Be King* (Dorothy L. Sayers), a radio play, for an evening of reading aloud with friends.
- Put all of your children's Easter-related books, tapes, DVDs, and videos in a basket so that they're handy for you and the children to pick up on the spur of the moment. This would include stories and information about Passover as well.
- Make use of the *Jesus* video (http://www.jesusvideo.org/) with your family and with friends who don't yet know Jesus personally.
- Set aside a special place for your family's devotional times, perhaps at the dining room table if that's where your Lenten candles are or beside your Resurrection Tree.
- Attend your church's services that are held during this season. Prepare yourself and your children for the focus and mood of each service.

    Palm Sunday—The people were praising with hosannas but were ready to turn against Jesus.

    Maundy Thursday—The Last Supper was a time of good-byes and preparation for separation. It would be the end of life together as the disciples had known it. Afterward in the Garden, Jesus' prayer was heart-wrenching, and his disciples deserted him, first in sleep and then by running away. Judas betrayed him, and Peter denied him during the trial and following persecution.

Good Friday—We see Jesus carrying his cross, and we imagine his pain. We hear his words from the cross. We shudder at his death and feel the weight of our own responsibility.

Easter—Hallelujah! Jesus has triumphed over death!

I have been crucified with Christ. It is no longer I who live, but Christ who lives in me. And the life I now live in the flesh I live by faith in the Son of God, who loved me and gave himself for me.

(GALATIANS 2:20)

For I am not ashamed of the gospel, for it is the power of God for salvation to everyone who believes, to the Jew first and also to the Greek. For in it the righteousness of God is revealed from faith for faith, as it is written, "The righteous shall live by faith."

(ROMANS 1:16-17)

The Lord is risen!
The Lord is risen indeed!

DEUTERONOMY 4:9

Only take care, and keep your soul diligently, lest you forget the things that your eyes have seen, and lest they depart from your heart all the days of your life. Make them known to your children and your children's children.

TEN

WHAT NOW?

The spaghetti was gone and nothing was left of the mini-éclairs but crumbs. When I stood up, the rehearsal dinner guests—all of them family and special friends—leaned back in their metal folding chairs to hear what I'd say to our son Karsten and his bride, Shelly.

"Until now your parents have been the keepers of traditions for you. Now you are beginning your own home, and the time has come for us to be heritage-passers and for you to become the shapers of tradition in your own family. I have some gifts for you tonight to represent that transfer of responsibility and joy."

First I handed them a baby pandanus plant, the descendant of a parlor-sized tree that had been given to Karsten's grandmother seventy years and who-knows-how-many plant generations earlier. Next was a Noël Calendar, like the Advent calendar Karsten had grown up with. And there was the box of ornaments I had given to Karsten Christmas by Christmas all his life.

Then, moving around behind Shelly, I unfastened the silver chain from my neck and placed it around hers. Inside the Delft-painted locket were two treasures— a photo of toddler Karsten and a blond curl saved from his first haircut. The necklace was a favorite of mine, and I had always promised Karsten it would be his wife's someday. This was the day.

The last gift was a new book of old recipes. For months I had been transferring to my computer all my ragtag collection from stained index cards, crisp yellow newspaper clippings, and random cookbook pages. In the introduction, I wrote:

> It's a risky thing to give these recipes to you. For one thing, I don't want you to think there's anything "sanctified" about these recipes more than others you may try or prefer. For another, no two cooks ever prepare the same dish—even from the same recipe!

> I heard a story one time about a young woman who tried and tried to make the best mashed potatoes possible, but her husband always said they were not as good as his mother's. The wife went through every step imaginable to make them smooth and light and fluffy, but they were never the same as Mother's. Finally, they visited Mother, and she served the legendary mashed potatoes. "See!" sighed the contented son. "See how wonderful these lumps are in the potatoes."

> So, both of you, think of these recipes as family heirlooms. Some are used and enjoyed. Others are stored safely on a shelf somewhere, available if wanted, but otherwise pretty much forgotten.

Whether it's recipes or traditions or raising their own children, I don't expect my adult children to do things exactly as I do. I certainly don't do everything the way my parents did. But they laid a foundation for me.

I can remember my mother when she was younger than I am now. Has she really changed very much? And how have I come to be in the position she held then? All of my grandparents are dead. So is my father. My mother is now the oldest generation, and I've moved up to her former place.

Someday another generational shift will happen for all of us, and our children will be contemplating the same questions. So we need to ask ourselves:

- Am I preparing my children to be the "older generation"?
- How well am I doing at teaching them to value the most priceless and endless treasure of glorifying God and enjoying him forever?
- Am I myself glorifying God and enjoying him?

Answers to these questions must come from every area of our lives together. Through their years with us, our interaction with our children will show them who God is and how he acts. Let's shower them with love and discipline in the broadest sense and convey as much of God as they can understand at whatever age they are.

In this book we have paid special attention to the role of traditions, because they reach into so many corners of a family's life, shaping and reflecting our understanding of love, discipline, and God.

OLD TRADITIONS AND NEW

My goal is that we *evaluate* our traditions. It's not enough to do things just because that's the way we've always done them. We must think about our traditions. If an activity or custom says what we mean about God and our relationship with him, we keep it. Some we'll want to change, and some we'll want to set aside to make place for something new.

But *tradition* implies a long-established practice, doesn't it? So isn't *new tradition* an oxymoron? Maybe so, but every tradition got its start sometime. Why not with you? I'm praying that what you've read in this book will be a springboard to your own traditions—some old, some reworked, and some new. Dive from the ideas here into the traditions *you* choose and form to fit your home and your family in this chapter of life. Your celebrations shouldn't try to include every detail you've read here. They *should* have God at the center.

Let's just remind ourselves of what we're after:

- Remembering what God did for his people, for us, and
- giving glory to God for what he's done,
- so our children and their children will know him.

If we want our children to know him, it's not enough just to be "doing" the right activities or using the symbolism of God's Word and work. We must remember to be "talking of them when you are sitting in your house, and when you are walking by the way, and when you lie down, and when you rise" (Deuteronomy 11:19). Without the verbal part, our traditions will become unfocused—beautiful, maybe—but without much point.

Value Even in Rituals Without a Focus

It is worth mentioning, though, that even in traditions that seem shallow, God releases glimmers of his presence. A friend of mine wrote:

> I grew up in a troubled, angry, and unpredictable family. One thing proved a small but weighty anchor for me: family holiday traditions. We didn't have Norman Rockwell holidays; ours were a much less funny version of The Honeymooners. But a base of security was laid down for me in the predictable cycle of heart-shaped Jello for Valentine's Day and French toast with thread sewn through the bread slices (April Fool!) and Easter baskets and Thanksgiving salad in that special bowl and Christmas decorations long, long past their prime but welcomed every December. No matter what else was going on, these traditions went on, and they strengthened me. I counted on them, and they were there, year in and year out. It wasn't enough, of course, but it was something, and God used it for my good in the midst of the pain.
>
> Red heart-shaped Jello, for crying out loud. Such a little thing. But red heart-shaped Jello year after year after year after year after year was something else entirely.

"It wasn't enough" she writes, "but it was something, and God used it for my good." Year after year after year the traditions were there, a shadow of our God who is rock-steady and dependable year after year after year. When God created seasons and memories and celebrations—traditions—he knew our need for security. And he knew that even paltry red Jello year after year can provide enough steadiness to keep us going until we find our only real security in him.

Value of God-centered Ritual

But how much more of God there is to find when we are on the lookout, when we shape our "everyday" and "especially" around him. God will show himself in special and new ways when we celebrate him. He will use our celebrations, our traditions, to stoke our heart's fire for him.

I used to run among the lightning bugs with my cousins while the adults talked in the dark on the front porch. That's history. Now my cousins and I are far older than our parents were then. Our parents are dying—the ones from whom we received our earthly heritage.

As they leave us, I feel myself more and more tuned in to the essential in my life. *The essential* is that the eyes of my heart be focused on the Author of the universe so that I celebrate the world and history as he's written it.

Then I turn from the generation who came before me and look toward the children who come after me. I want the story they live to resonate with the history written by that great Author of the universe. It is my heart's desire that they love God and enjoy him forever so that they will love the future he's already written.

Dear Noël, Walter, Travie, Juliette, Gwynn, Christa, Pamela, Rolfe, and Garnett,

I pray that I will be lucid and able to care for myself until the Lord calls me home. Pray with me that this will be so. Isn't our God good, and his continued blessings follow me regularly.

I love you all with a love that I have no vocabulary for. Only one person on this earth stands above you, and that person is your mother.

Each of you as a child has climbed into my lap, laid your head on my shoulder, and said, "Daddy, wipe the tears away." And when I wiped them away, you would relax and rest in peace. I wish I could wipe those tears away now and continuously, but there comes a time when your earthly father cannot fulfill this office, and you have to put your total dependence upon our heavenly Father and the Lord Jesus Christ.

I thank God for choosing you and yours for our family.

Our love and prayers for you all continue.

Dad

It is not from us that our children will receive their Heirloom. Only God can give himself to those who receive the inheritance. But we can praise the Lord that he allows us be part of his plan for bringing his children to himself, that he uses us to reveal to our children the beauty of our Heirloom—God.

May the ceremonies of our
homes be true ceremony—
from him,
because of him,
pointing toward him,
honoring him,
thanking him.
Amen.

The Family: Together in God's Presence

By John and Noël Piper

SOME THOUGHTS ON WORSHIP
from John

God-centered worship is supremely important in the life of our church. We approach the Sunday morning worship hour with great seriousness and earnestness and expectancy. We try to banish all that is flippant or trivial or chatty.

Not all services are this way. Sunday morning is the Mount of Transfiguration—the awesome place of glory and speechlessness. Sunday or Wednesday evening is the Mount of Olives—the familiar spot for conversation with the Lord and each other.

In this article, we hope to do two things: 1) demonstrate that parents (or some responsible adult) should bring little children to the Sunday morning worship service rather than send them to a "children's church"; 2) give some practical advice about how to do it.

We don't claim that our way of worshiping is the only valid way. Not all our ideas may fit with the way another church does it. For example, we don't have a children's sermon as part of our Sunday morning service. It would be fun for the children, but in the long run would weaken the spiritual intensity of our worship. To everything there is a season. And we believe that, for at least one hour a week, we should sustain a maximum intensity of moving reverence.

THE BIGGEST STUMBLING BLOCK

There are several reasons why we urge parents to bring their children to worship. But these arguments will not carry much weight with parents who do not love to worship God.

The greatest stumbling block for children in worship is that their parents do not cherish the hour. Children can feel the difference between duty and delight. Therefore, the first and most important job of a parent is to fall in love with the worship of God. You can't impart what you don't possess.

TOGETHERNESS

Worshiping together counters the contemporary fragmentation of families. Hectic American life leaves little time for significant togetherness. It is hard to overestimate the good influence of families doing valuable things together week in and week out, year in and year out.

Worship is the most valuable thing a human can do. The cumulative effect of 650 worship services spent with Mom and Dad between the ages of four and seventeen is incalculable.

CATCH THE SPIRIT

Parents have the responsibility to teach their children by their own example the meaning and value of worship. Therefore, parents should want their children with them in worship so that the children can catch the spirit and form of their parents' worship.

Children should see how Mom and Dad bow their heads in earnest prayer during the prelude and other nondirected times. They should see how Mom and Dad sing praise to God with joy in their faces and how they listen hungrily to his Word. They should catch the spirit of their parents meeting the living God.

Something seems wrong when parents want to take their children in the formative years and put them with other children and other adults to form their attitude and behavior in worship. Parents should be jealous to model for their children the tremendous value they put on reverence in the presence of Almighty God.

NOT AN EXCESSIVE EXPECTATION

To sit still and be quiet for an hour or two on Sunday is not an excessive expectation for a healthy, normal six-year-old who has been taught to obey his parents. It requires a measure of discipline, but that is precisely what we want to encourage parents to impart to their children in the first five years.

Thus the desire to have children in the worship service is part of a broader concern that children be reared so that they are "submissive and respectful in every way" (1 Timothy 3:4 RSV).

Children can be taught in the first five years of life to obey their father and mother when they say, "Sit still and be quiet." In general, parents' helplessness to control their children should not be solved by alternative services but by a renewal of discipline in the home.

NOT EVERYTHING GOES OVER THEIR HEADS

Children absorb a tremendous amount that is of value. And this is true even if they say they are bored.

Music and words become familiar. The message of the music starts to sink in. The form of the service comes to feel natural. The choir makes a special impression with a kind of music the children may hear at no other time. Even if most of the sermon goes over their heads, experience shows that children hear and remember remarkable things.

The content of the prayers and songs and sermon gives parents unparalleled opportunities to teach their children the great truths of our faith. If parents would only learn to query their children after the service and then explain things, the children's capacity to participate would soar.

Not everything children experience has to be put on their level in order to do them good. Some things must be. But not everything.

For example, to learn a new language you can go step by step from alphabet to vocabulary to grammar to syntax. Or you can take a course where you dive in over your head, and all you hear is the language you don't know. Most language teachers would agree that the latter is by far the most effective.

Sunday worship service is not useless to children just because much of it goes over their heads. They can and will grow into this new language faster than we think—if positive and happy attitudes are fostered by the parents.

A Sense of Awe

There is a sense of solemnity and awe that children should experience in the presence of God. This is not likely to happen in children's church. Is there such a thing as children's thunder or children's lightning or the crashing of the sea "for children"?

A deep sense of the unknown and the mysterious can rise in the soul of a sensitive child in solemn worship—if his parents are going hard after God themselves. A deep moving of the magnificence of God can come to the young, tender heart through certain moments of great hymns or "loud silence" or authoritative preaching. These are of immeasurable value in the cultivation of a heart that fears and loves God.

We do not believe that children who have been in children's church for several years between the ages of six and twelve will be more inclined or better trained to enjoy worship than if they had spent those years at the side of their parents. In fact, the opposite is probably the case.

It will probably be harder to acclimate a ten- or twelve-year-old to a new worship service than a five- or six-year-old. The cement is much less wet, and vast possibilities of shaping the impulses of the heart are gone.

Some Practical Suggestions
from Noël

When our four sons grew to be young men, we assumed that the worship-training chapter of our life had ended. But God has wonderful surprises. Our youngest son was twelve when we adopted our daughter, who was just a couple of months old. So our experience with young children in the pew started about thirty years ago and will continue awhile longer.

GETTING STARTED STEP BY STEP

We discovered that the very earliest "school" for worship is in the home—when we help a baby be quiet for just a moment while we ask God's blessing on our meal; when a toddler is sitting still to listen to a Bible storybook; when a child is learning to pay attention to God's Word and to pray during family devotional times.

At church, even while our children were still nursery-aged, I began to help them take steps toward eventual regular attendance in Sunday morning worship service. I used other gatherings as a training ground—baptisms, choir concerts, missionary videos, or other special events that would grab the attention of a three-year-old. I'd "promote" these to the child as something exciting and grown up. The occasional special attendance gradually developed into regular evening attendance, while at the same time we were beginning to attempt Sunday mornings more and more regularly.

I've chosen not to use the church's child care as an escape route when the service becomes long or the child gets restless. I don't want to communicate that you go to a service as long as it seems interesting, and then you can go play. And I wanted to avoid a pattern that might reinforce the idea that all of the service is good up until the preaching of God's Word—then you can leave.

Of course, there are times when a child gets restless or noisy, despite a parent's best efforts. I pray for the understanding of the people around me and try to deal with the problem unobtrusively. But if the child won't be quiet or still, I take him or her out—for the sake of quick discipline and for the sake of the other worshipers. Then I have to decide whether we'll slip back into service or stay in the area reserved for parents with young children. It depends on how responsive the child seems and whether there's an appropriate moment in the flow of the service. If we stay in the "family area" outside the sanctuary, I help my child sit quietly as if we were still in the sanctuary.

By the time they are four years old, our children assume that they'll be at all the regular weekly services with us.

PREPARATION ALL WEEK LONG

Your anticipation and conversation before and after service and during the week will be important in helping your child learn to love worship and to behave well in service.

Help your children become acquainted with your pastor. Let them shake hands with him at the door and be greeted by him. Talk about who the worship leaders are; call them by name. Suggest that your child's Sunday school teacher invite the pastor to spend a few minutes with the children if your church's Sunday morning schedule allows for that.

If you know what the Scripture passage will be for the coming Sunday, read it together several times during the week. A little one's face really lights up when he hears familiar words from the pulpit.

Talk about what is "special" this week: a trumpet solo, a friend singing, a missionary speaker from a country you have been praying for.

Sometimes you can take the regular elements of the service and make them part of the anticipation. "We've been reading about Joseph. What do you think the pastor will say about him?" "What might the choir be singing this morning?" "Maybe we can sit next to our handicapped friend and help him with his hymnbook so he can worship better too."

There are two additional and important pre-service preparations for us: a pen and notepad for "Sunday notes" and a trip to the restroom (leaving the service is highly discouraged).

WHAT HAPPENS DURING SERVICE?

First, I let a child who wants a worship folder have one. It helps a child feel like a participant in the service. And quietly, before service begins, I may point to the different parts of the service listed in the folder.

During the service, we all sit or stand along with rest of the congregation. I share my Bible or hymnal or worship folder with my little one, because use of these is an important part of the service.

The beginning of the sermon is the signal for "note-taking" to begin. (I want a child's activities to be related to the service. So we don't bring library books to read. I do let a very young child look at pictures in his Bible if he can do it quietly.) Note-taking doesn't mean just scribbling, but "taking notes" on a special pad used just for the service.

"Taking notes" grows up as the child does. At first he draws pictures of what he hears in the sermon. Individual words or names trigger individual pictures. You might pick out a word that will be used frequently in the sermon; have the child listen carefully and make a check mark in his "notes" each time he hears the word.

Later he may want to copy letters or words from the Scripture passage for the morning. When spelling comes easier, he will write words and then phrases he hears in the sermon. Before you might expect it, he may be outlining the sermon and noting whole concepts.

Goals and Requirements

My training for worship has three main goals:

1. That children learn early and as well as they can to worship God heartily.
2. That parents be able to worship.
3. That families cause no distraction to the people around them.

So there are certain expectations that I teach the young ones and expect of the older ones:

- Sit or stand or close their eyes when the service calls for it.
- Sit up straight and still—not lounging or fidgeting or crawling around, but respectful toward God and the other worshipers nearby.
- Keep bulletin papers and Bible and hymnal pages as quiet as possible.
- Stay awake. Taking notes helps. (I did allow the smallest ones to sleep, but they usually didn't need to!)
- Look toward the worship leaders in the front. No people-gazing or clock-watching.
- If you can read fast enough, sing along with the printed words. At least keep your eyes on the words and try to think them. If you can't read yet, listen very hard.

Creating an Environment in the Pew

For my part, I try to create an environment in our pew that makes worship easier. In past years, I would sit between whichever two were having the most trouble with each other that day. We choose seats where we can see the front better while seated, not kneeling on the pew; kneeling leads to squirming and blocks the view of others).

Each child has a Bible, offering money, and worship folder at hand; so he doesn't have to scramble and dig during the worship time. During the prelude, if I notice in the bulletin something unusual for which we need to be prepared (a responsive reading or congregational prayers, for example), I quietly point it out to a child who is old enough to participate.

Afterward

When the service has ended, my first words are praise to the child who has behaved well. In addition to the praise, I might also mention one or two things that we both hope will be better next time.

But what if there has been disregard of our established expectations and little attempt to behave? The first thing that happens following the service is a silent and immediate trip to the most private place we can find. Then the deserved words are spoken and consequences administered or promised.

CLOSENESS AND WARMTH

On the rare occasions when my pastor-husband can sit with the rest of us, the youngest one climbs right into his lap—and is more attentive and still than usual. What a wonderful thing for a young mind to closely associate the closeness and warmth of a parent's lap with special God-times.

A child beyond the lap stage can get the same feeling from being next to his parent or from an arm around the shoulder or an affectionate hand on the knee.

The setting of the tight family circle focusing toward God will be a nonverbal picture growing richer and richer in the child's mind and heart as he matures in appreciation for his family and in awe at the greatness of God.

PUBLISHED ORIGINALLY IN *THE STANDARD*, MARCH 1986. REVISED, NOVEMBER 1999.

NOTES

1. From a sermon given on May 11, 1993, © Desiring God Ministries. Website: www.desiringGOD.org

2. Carine MacKenzie, *My First Book of Questions and Answers* (Ross-shire, Scotland: Christian Focus Publications, 2001). In a foreword Douglas Kelly writes that this book "is organized so that the theological concepts follow each other in proper order, much like its model, the Westminster Shorter Catechism."

3. Noël Piper, "Betsey Stockton, 1789-1865: From Slavery to the World," audiotape available through Desiring God Ministries, www.desiringGOD.org or 888-346-4700 (toll-free).

4. For more ideas, see Noël Piper, "Home-Grown World Christians." It is available through Desiring God Ministries, www.desiringGOD.org or 888-346-4700 (toll-free).

5. U.S. Center for World Mission, 1605 E. Elizabeth St., Pasadena CA 91104-2721, or http://www.uscwm.org.

6. Milo Shannon-Thornberry, *The Alternate Celebrations Catalogue* (New York: The Pilgrim Press, 1982), 14.

7. St. Augustine, *Confessions,* quoted in *Documents of the Christian Church*, ed. Henry Bettenson (London: Oxford University Press, 1967), 54.

8. John Piper, *Desiring God: Meditations of a Christian Hedonist* (Sisters, Ore.: Multnomah, 1996), 143.

9. Barbara Robinson, *The Best Christmas Pageant Ever* (New York: Harper Trophy, 1972), 73-74.

10. For more information or to order a Noël Calendar, visit www.desiringGOD.org or call 888-346-4700 (toll-free).

11. "Never in January" can be read in full at www.desiringGOD.org. Follow the "Noël Piper" links.

12. John Piper, *A Hunger for God* (Wheaton, Ill.: Crossway Books, 1997), 18, 19, 20.

13. Noël Piper, *Lenten Lights*, a booklet of devotions for use alone or with Lenten candles. For more information or to order, visit www.desiringGod.org or call 888-346-4700 (toll-free).

Noël Calendar
Advent Calendar—A Family Tradition for the Generations

This Advent calendar, designed by Noël Piper, has become a treasured tradition of the Pipers and many others. Each day in December, the story begins:

Jesus is the greatest Treasure of all. This is the story of how he came to us.

Long ago God made a promise about a little town named Bethlehem. He said, "O Bethlehem . . . From you shall come forth for me one who is to be ruler in Israel." Jesus is the King that God promised to send.

One time, a long time ago, in Bethlehem there was a place called a stable. In the stable there was a manger, filled with hay . . .

After hearing these words, a child removes the manger from its calendar square and places it in position on the top half of the banner. That ends the first day's story. On each subsequent day until Christmas, the story starts again at the beginning and stretches a little further. And each day one more figure is added to the illustration of the Nativity.

As they have heard the story day after day, young children have learned the true CHRISTmas story. Then, as they've grown older, they can't imagine Christmas without the Noël Calendar. One newlywed wrote: "My sister and I looked forward to the Advent calendar every December. I just ordered one for Steve and me and any possible future additions to our family."

So, as well as being a Christ-centered Christmas gift, the Noël Calendar is an excellent wedding or baby gift year-round, helping families focus on their true Treasure.

Set includes a 21" x 27" burlap banner, 25 figures, a segmented dowel, and a laminated brochure with instructions and the Advent story.

For more information or to order, contact Desiring God Ministries (see page 120).

RESOURCES

FROM NOËL PIPER

Resources in this section, except for *Most of All, Jesus Loves You,* may be ordered from DesiringGod.org; follow the "Noël Piper" links or call toll-free 888-346-4700.

"The Family: Together in God's Presence." Available to read online or may be ordered in brochure format.

"Home-Grown World Christians." Available to read online or may be ordered in brochure format.

Lenten Lights. Booklet of devotions for the season before Easter.

Most of All, Jesus Loves You (Wheaton: Crossway Books, 2004). The story of a loving bedtime tradition for toddlers and preschoolers.

"Never in January." Thoughts about personal Bible reading in the midst of a busy life. Available to read online.

READING AND DEVOTIONAL HELPS

Fighter Verses Memorization System, Children Desiring God. Order from DesiringGod.org; follow the "Children Desiring God" and "Bible Memorization" links.

Green, Steve. *Hide 'Em in Your Heart,* vols. 1 and 2. Cassettes or CDs of songs for Bible memory. Sparrow Records.

Hughes, Barbara, ed. *Devotions for Ministry Wives* (Grand Rapids: Zondervan, 2002). Ninety devotions, including several by Noël Piper, for any woman trying to live a life of ministry.

Hunt, Gladys. *Honey for a Child's Heart* (Grand Rapids: Zondervan, 2002). Ideas for reading with children and encouraging them to love reading.

Schooland, *Leading Little Ones to God* (Grand Rapids: Eerdmans, 1981). Devotional book for preschool and young school-aged children.

MacKenzie, Carine, *My 1st Book of Questions and Answers* (Ross-shire, Scotland: Christian Focus Publications, 2001). Catechism for children.

Becoming World Christians (a small sample)

Mission Frontiers, U.S. Center for World Mission, 1605 Elizabeth St., Pasadena CA 91104-2721. Subscribe or read online this bimonthly publication: www.missionfrontiers.org.

Global Prayer Digest, U.S. Center for World Mission, Frontier Fellowship, 1605 Elizabeth St., Pasadena, CA 91104-2721. Subscribe or read online this daily guide for praying daily for the unreached peoples: www.global-prayer-digest.org.

Joni and Friends, P.O. Box 3333, Agoura Hills, CA 91376. An international ministry whose mission is "to evangelize and disciple people affected by disabilities." Find help and opportunities: joniandfriends.org.

Bible Story Cassettes

Dear Noël,

You write that your children listened to stories on tape while they were too young to read. Could you recommend some good, sound children's Bible story recordings?

Thank you.

Dear friend,

That's a good question and difficult to answer. The sets we used are out of print, and it's hard now to find good options. Perhaps publishers think kids are too visually oriented to be interested in audio.

These are ones that we've used and liked:

- *Stories That Live,* a large series of books and tapes produced by Peter Enns.
- *A Few Who Dared to Trust God,* a set of five cassettes produced by the American Bible Society.
- *The Word and Song Bible,* books and tapes, ed. Steve Elkins (Broadman & Holman, 2000).

I'd suggest typing those titles into your Internet search engine. You might find one used or back in print. Or your search may uncover some other treasure. (When you find something good, I'd like to hear about it!)

When buying something unfamiliar from a Christian business that presumably cares about the biblical faithfulness of its merchandise, I'd ask up front if there's a way to preview audio before buying or if it's possible to return opened tapes or CDs if they are not as clearly biblical as the packaging indicates.

Here are some of the basics I'm looking for in audio for pre-readers.

• A Bible story told without added details or characters;

• Presentation of God as the central character;

• Appropriate respect given to the Word of God;

• Less important but helpful to a younger child is that stories be narrated rather than dramatized.

If you can't find what you want or simply want the Bible time experience to be more intimate, why not make a recording yourself from your child's favorite Bible storybooks?

Blessings on you and your family as you grow together in God's Word.

Noël Piper

⁑ desiringGod

If you would like to ponder further the vision of God and life presented in this book, we at Desiring God would love to serve you. We have produced hundreds of resources to help you grow in your passion for God and help you spread that passion to others.

At our website, desiringGod.org, you'll find almost all of the resources John Piper has written and preached, including more than 30 books. We've made over 25 years of his sermons available free for you to read, listen to, download, and in some cases watch online. In addition, you can access hundreds of articles, listen to our daily internet radio program, find out where John Piper is speaking, learn about our conferences, discover our God-centered children's curricula, and browse our online store.

John Piper receives no royalties from the books he writes and no remuneration from Desiring God. These funds are all reinvested into our gospel-spreading efforts. DG also has a whatever-you-can-afford policy for the materials we sell, designed for individuals with limited discretionary funds. If you'd like more information about this policy, please contact us at the address or phone number below.

We exist to help you treasure Jesus Christ above all things because he is most glorified in you when you are most satisfied in him. Let us know how we can serve you!

Desiring God
2601 East Franklin Avenue
Minneapolis, MN 55406-1103

888.346.4700 (phone)
612.338.4372 (fax)
Email: mail@desiringGod.org
Web: www.desiringGod.org

OUR TRADITIONS

OUR TRADITIONS

OUR TRADITIONS

OUR TRADITIONS

OUR TRADITIONS

OUR TRADITIONS

OUR TRADITIONS

OUR TRADITIONS